The Covert Side of Initiation

By Virgil

FALCON BOOKS
PUBLISHING
2018

Other Titles by Virgil

The Spirit of Magic: Rediscovering the Heart of Our Sacred Art (Falcon Books Publishing 2017)

The Elemental Equilibrium: Notes on the Foundation of Magical Adepthood (Falcon Books Publishing 2017)

Future Publications

Awake in the Starlight (Falcon Books Publishing)

The Covert Side of Initiation

By Virgil

Falcon Books
Publishing
2018

Copyright © 2018 by Virgil
All rights reserved. This book or any portion thereof may not be reproduced or used in any manner whatsoever without the express written permission of the publisher except for the use of brief quotations in a book review or scholarly journal.
First Printing: 2018

Cover Design by Rostik Balash

Falcon Books Publishing
www.falconbookspublishing.com
Copyright © 2018 Virgil
All rights reserved.

ISBN: 978-986-94925-3-9

Dedication

This book is dedicated to two friends of mine…

To Noel for being the kindest person I have ever met, and for partnering with me over the summer to do transportation research.

And

To Matt, who does not like jelly beans, for teaching me how much more enjoyable life can be if you have a spontaneous personality, and for coming up with the box design that kept Team Jacob's bridge from deflecting more than two inches.

Table of Contents

Dedication..v
Table of Contents..vii
Acknowledgments..ix
Preface..xiii
Introduction..xv
Abbreviations..xvii
Chapter 1: Shoshin..1
Chapter 2: The Tower..5
Chapter 3: The Intent Key..12
Chapter 4: Mature Speech..16
Chapter 5: An Excerpt from a Speech-Regulation Journal.....25
Chapter 6: Malkuth..32
Chapter 7: Present-Mindedness....................................39
Chapter 8: Notes on Self-Transformation......................49
Chapter 9: Kindness..64
Chapter 10: Saturn..71
Chapter 11: Taking on New Roles................................80
Chapter 12: Compassion...87
Chapter 13: Melons...95
Chapter 14: A Few More Things..................................101
Chapter 15: Wisdom..111
Chapter 16: Reading..118
Chapter 17: Charisma..124
Bonus Content: A Walk Down Memory Lane..................135
Works Cited, Referenced, or Consulted........................201

Acknowledgments

"This soil is as strong as nails."
~*Kevin*

This is always the most fun part of a book to write...

There are many individuals in my life I owe my deepest gratitude towards, either because they helped me write this book, or for some other reason that has nothing to do with my writing career.

I want to start by thanking those readers who have been with me from the very beginning. In particular, I must thank Melanie Laskowski, Sapnali Chetia, Ewen Barling, Cass VanBaal, Eden VanBaal, Wayne O'Boogie, Eduardo Ballena, Eric Summers, Gabriel Moreira, Pakpoom Poolsong, Ioan Rocsoreanu, Lucas Augusto, Jacob Scully, Guido Cesano, Marc Pugliese, Eric Willis, Steve Vadney, R.H. Andrew, Mario Kulash, Nathan Quick, Johannes Kul, Colter Davis, Philip Raquinel, Fabio Salvi's Tricks, Charles Freeman, Nenad Vasin, Devin Kelly, Mahazou Mahaman, D.C. Voss, and everyone else who has supported my writing efforts. You guys are truly a blessing to me, and I wouldn't be able to do what I do without your encouragement and feedback.

In addition, I must thank Tanya Robinson for publishing this book. The fact that a text document on my computer has turned into a book people around the world are reading is incredible to think about. Thank you for making this happen.

I must also thank William Mistele for corresponding with me, for producing writings that will guide aspiring magicians forever, and for working magically to establish peace and justice in this world.

I must thank Rawn Clark for his clear and concise explanations of important magical concepts, for showing me what it means to be a respectful person via his online interactions, and for sharing TMO with the world.

I must thank Frater Acher for showing me that I am a high ranking member of the Order of Unlearning, I have been struggling to climb down the pyramid for a long time. Progress is slow, but I am determined to make it to the bottom.

I must thank Josephine McCarthy for helping me come to a better understanding of what balance is and what service is, and for exposing many of the flaws in the most common modern approaches to magic. I know your writings will help future generations of magicians avoid the pitfalls and traps that consumed many of the serious but misguided aspiring magicians of the past.

I must thank Crystalf Maibach for the insights about esotericism he has given me during our private conversations, for his feedback about my previous two books, and for the thoughts about magic he shares on his blog.

I must thank my friend Kevin for taking me to see *Star Wars: The Last Jedi,* and for pointing out that the pins were still in the shear box during that one direct shear test when we were wondering why the gauges weren't moving.

I must thank my friend Rachel, who loves economics and chemistry, for her book recommendations and for teaching me how to do regressions in MATLAB.

I must thank my friend Roberto for showing me the diamond shaped base of his cantilever and for discussing the logic behind it with me. Honestly, it never occurred to me to orient the block of wood that way. It makes me wonder what other possibilities I've been blind to in all of my past projects.

I must thank my Slytherin friend Chanel for showing me that it's ok if your patronus keeps changing. Honestly, I rarely know what mine is with any degree of certainty. It seems to depend on my mood. Do you like jelly beans though? Apparently Matt doesn't, but I can't seem to figure out why.

I must thank Ng Mui for creating Wing Chun and Natalie Portman for being an amazing actress.

I must thank my friend Victoria for reminding me that there are equations that give the relationship between the average degree of consolidation and the non-dimensional time factor. I was staring at the table for a long time wondering what I was supposed to do if the degree of consolidation I was working with wasn't in it. Also, thanks for doing all of the AutoCAD drawings of the bridge.

I must thank my friend Matt for agreeing with me that the colored pencils we were using to color Victoria's AutoCAD drawings looked like Darth Maul's light saber. Also, thank you for telling me the story about how you got banned from your school's library. It was entertaining.

I must thank my friend Noel for writing the MATLAB code to calculate the emissions, for learning how to do that spatial join thing in QGIS so I didn't have to, for creating the entire poster, for doing the engineering drawings of the warped mirror, and for too many other things to list.

I must thank my friend Austin for the wonderful poster presentation he gave to Noel and me about the axial lab. It gave my life a whole new sense of meaning and helped me reach enlightenment. Also, thank you for alerting me to the fact that bird poop on solar panels is real problem. This fascinating tidbit of information will stay with me until I leave my current physical body and depart for my next life.

I must thank my friend Gabe for driving me to center every week. I can't wait to read all of the literary fiction you will go on to write, and see the ways you will come up with to prevent our beaches from eroding.

Finally, I'd like to thank everyone who taught me that you make a bigger positive impact on the world when you express your views honestly than when you refrain from doing so out of fear that you will offend the narrow-minded.

"I will share with you a secret. No hope can be found in a life devoid of peace. Now that you know, I will ask. To how many lives have you brought peace and to how many hearts hope? If you can but do, joy will be the reward. Bring a smile to a lonely heart and your name the dove will always cry."

~The Codex of Love

"It is one thing to have a good heart. But to change wrong to right you will need a good heart in combination with great power."

~William Mistele

Preface

The word "maturity" appears in IIH thirty-two times. Throughout the text of the book, Bardon repeatedly asserts that a magician must be mature, and that the rate the student progresses through his training depends on his maturity. In Step 6, he asserts that the degree to which a magician can master the elements depends on his maturity. In Step 7, he asserts that the quality of the magician's clairvoyance depends on his maturity. In Step 8, he asserts that how far into the inner planes a magician can travel via the technique of mental wandering depends on his maturity.

From all of this, it's not unreasonable to conclude that a concise and practical guide to maturity and all of the various processes involved in becoming mature is what the Bardon community needs the most. Am I the person who is the most qualified to write this guide? Nope. However, because the Bardon community is sorely in need of such a guide, and because no one has yet written such a guide, I decided to take a crack at it.

Think of the process of becoming mature as a puzzle. Bardon doesn't give us the puzzle. Although he tells us it's important, he still leaves us to find the pieces ourselves. If we find all of the pieces and put them together, then we'll end up with a complete picture of what it takes to become mature. The fourth through fifteenth chapters of this book contain some of the pieces of the puzzle. They don't contain all of the pieces, but they contain enough for you to figure out what you need to do to get started on the process of becoming mature. That's enough to satisfy me. The process of becoming mature is complex and does not happen overnight. What's important to me is that you know enough to get started. Maybe at some future time another magician will come along and give you the missing pieces of the puzzle that I did not include in this book, either because I overlooked them or just did not know about them. Until then, this book should suffice.

Introduction

"There is nothing occult which shall not be known; there is nothing concealed which shall not be revealed."

~Eliphas Levi

Imagine an iceberg. The iceberg has a tip that everyone can see, but most of the iceberg is underwater and hidden from view. If magical training were an iceberg, practicing magical exercises to develop magical skills and abilities would be the tip. That's because anyone can see the tip. Similarly, anyone can see that practicing magical exercises is a part of magical training. It's just an obvious fact.

However, the tip of an iceberg is not the entirety of the iceberg. There is so much more that is hidden beneath the surface. Similarly, there are many other parts of magical training besides practicing magical exercises. Because these other parts of magical training are hidden from those who are not sincere students of magic, I refer to them collectively as the "covert side" of magical training or initiation.

The hidden part of an iceberg is bigger than the tip and supports the tip. Similarly, the covert side of magical training is bigger than and supports the overt side. What are the aspects of magical training that form its covert side?

Many of these aspects center on maturity. When you practice magical exercises, you gain magical skills and abilities. However, if you use these magical skills and abilities immaturely, you can inflict a lot of suffering upon others, accumulate a great deal of negative karma for yourself, and destroy the Balance and the Pattern of your life and the environment in which you dwell. It's unsurprising, then, that Divine Providence often places obstacles and restrictions in the way of aspiring magicians to halt their progress until they have reached the level of maturity needed to advance.

This is why the most important parts of magical training center on becoming more mature. This book is about those parts. In the process of becoming mature, you will learn to speak maturely, treat others with kindness, fulfill your responsibilities, develop different aspects of yourself by taking on different roles, open your mind and heart, learn the lessons contained in unpleasant experiences, and acquire wisdom. You can sit in a chair meditating, visualizing, and accumulating magical energies all day, but you will never come anywhere close to adepthood if that's all you do. What indicates a magician's true level of advancement is not how much energy he can accumulate, how clairvoyant he is, or how many rituals he has performed. It's how mature he is.

Abbreviations

ABC – A Bardon Companion

IIH – Initiation into Hermetics

KTQ – The Key to the True Quabbalah

PITSOM – Problems in the Study of Magic[1]

PME – The Practice of Magical Evocation

TRFSS – Ten Rules for Spiritual Seekers[2]

TRFSS(EV) – Ten Rules for Spiritual Seekers (Extended Version)[3]

Chapter 1: Shoshin

Throughout the text of IIH, Bardon continually emphasizes the importance of practicing regularly and seriously. He does this for good reason. If you don't practice your magical exercises regularly, or if you don't practice them seriously, you won't make any progress in the work of mastering them. What Bardon neglects to point out is that if you don't approach your training in the mental state of shoshin, you still won't make any progress, regardless of how persistently or how seriously you practice your exercises.

People who begin the work of IIH with no previous experience with esotericism, occultism, or magic have an enormous advantage over those who begin the work of IIH after years of esoteric, occult, and magical studies. This is because the minds of the former default to shoshin, while the latter must make a conscious effort to enter shoshin and remain in this mental state. This can be difficult. In a nutshell, shoshin means having no preconceived notions.

Shotokan karate is a martial art. Figure skating is not a martial art. In fact, Shotokan and figure skating are two essentially different disciplines. Imagine that someone who desires to learn figure skating mistakenly believes Shotokan to be a form of figure skating. As a result, he begins learning Shotokan. In the process of learning Shotokan, he thinks of each exercise as a figure skating exercise and approaches it the way he would approach a figure skating exercise instead of a martial arts exercise. Clearly, as a result of his preconceived notion that Shotokan is a form of figure skating, such a person would never master Shotokan. Furthermore, even if such an individual did by some miracle master Shotokan, he would never be able to apply this martial art practically. If he is physically assaulted by hooligans, he would not use his art to defend himself because he would think it only works in an ice skating rink and is only good for impressing audiences.

Many western magical traditions teach their students that magic and yoga are synonymous. Imagine that a student who has studied one of these traditions later discovers the Bardon system and attempts to work through IIH. Because Bardon states that his system is one of magic, and because the student has been taught that magic is yoga, he believes that the Bardon system is a system of yoga. Therefore, he approaches his magical training as if he were training to be a yogi instead of a magician. This student is in the same situation as the Shotokan student who thought he was learning to figure skate. If he had begun studying the Bardon system in shoshin, he would have had a better chance of learning what the word "magic" means in the Bardon system and approaching his training correctly.

Many people assume, based on their prior reading and experiences, that any exercise which involves breathing is pranayama. Therefore, they assume Bardon's conscious breathing exercise is pranayama and when they study his instructions in an effort to understand them, they do so while holding onto the idea that the exercise is a pranayama exercise. Needless to say, any understanding they do arrive at is distorted at best. If such people were to read and study Bardon's conscious breathing instructions while in shoshin, they would have a better chance of understanding this exercise.

Similarly, many people think that every magical act involves visualization. As a result of this preconceived notion about magical acts, they assume conscious eating and conscious breathing involve visualization. They practice these exercises incorrectly and derive little benefit, if any at all, from their efforts. Again, had they read Bardon's instructions for these exercises while in shoshin, they would have had a better chance of understanding these exercises and practicing them correctly. Neither conscious eating nor conscious breathing involves visualization, just focused intent.

Some people know a lot about how magical training is formulated, structured, and viewed in other systems. Problems arise when these people assume that this also means they know how magical training is formulated, structured, and viewed in the Bardon system. If this assumption causes them to neglect to study the way magical training is formulated, structured, and viewed in the Bardon system, then they will never understand magical training as it is formulated, structured, and viewed in the Bardon system. This will prevent them from successfully working through the Bardon system.

When a Shotokan black belt begins training in Kyokushin, he starts as a white belt, not as a black belt. Shotokan and Kyokushin are closely related, yet not the same. Soto uke is performed differently in the two styles. When a Shotokan karateka performs soto uke, he focuses on turning his arm in a manner that deflects the opponent's power away from him. When a Kyokushin karateka performs soto uke, he focuses on angling his arm in such a way that it cuts into his opponent's attacking arm. From the outside, these two methods of blocking look identical, but the mechanics underlying them are very different. To learn to perform soto uke the way it is done in Kyokushin, the Shotokan karateka needs to forget what he knows about soto uke and enter shoshin while his Kyokushin sensei is teaching him the Kyokushin way of performing the block.

When a judo black belt begins training in Brazilian jiu-jitsu, he starts as a white belt, not as a black belt. The two fighting disciplines are again related, but not the same. In judo, the hip throw is done in such a way that the opponent lands on his shoulder because when done this way, it is easier to use the opponent's momentum to throw him. In Brazilian jiu-jitsu, the hip throw is done in such a way that the opponent lands on his butt. This is because if the opponent lands on his butt, it's harder for him to roll away and escape. From the outside, these two methods of performing a hip throw look similar, but they're not the same. To learn to perform a hip throw the way it is done in Brazilian jiu-jitsu, the judoka needs to forget what he knows about the hip throw and enter shoshin while his Brazilian jiu-jitsu instructor teaches him how the throw is done in Brazilian jiu-jitsu.

I could go on and on listing examples of preconceived notions and assumptions based on prior occult studies preventing people from understanding and correctly practicing the exercises of IIH. I think you get the point though. If you've studied magic or occultism in the past, you might think you know how to "balance the elements," or how to meditate, or what an adept is, or how the occult anatomy works. You certainly might know all of that from the perspective of some other magical training system, but that doesn't necessarily mean you know any of it from the perspective of the Bardon system. When you read through IIH, forget everything you think you know and let the text speak to you directly, rather than through the web of preconceived ideas and assumptions about magic you have built up in your mind. Only in this way can you really understand the instructions of IIH and ascertain the intent behind those instructions.

As far as magical training systems and forms of spirituality in general go, the Bardon system is very unique. Many of the attitudes, principles, ideals, and sources of inspiration that are central to other magical training systems and forms of spirituality are not relevant to the Bardonist. The standards of the Bardon system may be higher or lower than those of other magical training systems. Even when it comes to exercises that the Bardon system has in common with other magical training systems (e.g. visualization, meditation, mental wandering), these exercises are often approached in a different way that is unique to the Bardon system.

Outside knowledge can be useful on your journey to work through the Bardon system; however, you must understand that it can also get in the way. The first step towards mitigating this danger is to be aware of it. When you first begin working through the Bardon system, set that outside knowledge aside, enter shoshin, and view the Bardon system without the lenses and filters that this outside knowledge would create. When you have understood the Bardon system after viewing it in this way while working through it for some time, then go back to your outside knowledge. You will be in a better position to use that outside knowledge wisely without letting it get in your way.

Chapter 2: The Tower

Since this is a book about magical training, I want to begin with a few comments on magic, magical training, and magical training systems in order to ensure that we are on the same page. Different people often have very different views on these subjects, and thus, much confusion can arise when discussing them.

Few cards appear more ominous in a reading than the Tower. The Death card usually refers to a transformation of some sort, after all, this is essentially what death is in the hermetical sense. The Nine of Swords is often nicknamed the "nightmare card," yet the person who draws this card can take solace in the fact that nightmares are illusory. The Devil usually indicates one is stuck in an unfavorable position of some sort, but this does not mean that one is suffering. In addition, with some careful thought, it is usually a simple matter for the inquirer to figure out in what way she is stuck and to begin formulating a plan to become free.

The Tower card is a card of revelation. Imagine a slave who is dreaming that he is a high and mighty king. This is a pleasant dream, but at some point he must wake up. When he does, he will find that he is a lowly slave. The process of being struck by lightning and knocked down, as captured in the imagery of the Tower card, is like the process of the slave waking up and finding he is a lowly slave instead of a high king.

The lightning bolt of the Tower card wakes us up to the truth. Why then are people so afraid of this card? It's because a lot of the time, people are afraid of the truth.

Consider a hypothetical occultist—we'll call him Jake. Throughout the four decades Jake has been studying occultism, he has read hundreds of books on occultism, esotericism, mysticism, and magic. He has joined three different magical orders and has risen through the ranks of these orders until the point where he has become the leader of one and holds an adept position in the other two. Throughout his life, he has spent thousands of dollars furnishing his oratory and creating magical tools from the highest quality materials. He has also written a few books on magical subjects. Jake considers himself to be one of the greatest living adepts. However, despite all of this, he is a complete slave to his passions. He views any critical remark made against him as an unforgivable attack on his honor and immediately makes plans to avenge himself through as many petty ways as he can think of. He is irritable and impatient. He is arrogant and believes that when it comes to esoteric matters, there is nothing more for him to learn. Furthermore, he is dishonest and regularly tells lies about himself in order to appear grander than he really is.

This person is like the lowly slave that is dreaming that he is a high king. If you're an active member of the western esoteric community or some sub-branch of it, you've probably met a few people like Jake. Imagine if Jake were to learn one day that he is as far from being an adept as the human race is from building a working time machine. Jake would be devastated. This is why people fear the Tower. The Tower indicates that some kind of devastating revelation is going to happen.

Imagine that the tower in the Tower card is IIH. The bottom of the tower is Step 1. The top of the tower is Step 10. Some people climb to the top of the tower and then get blasted down. The truth is, they were never really at the top. The lightning bolt didn't knock them off the tower. The lightning bolt awakened them and caused them to realize they had yet to begin climbing.

Let's consider a hypothetical ineffective martial art that we'll call Bogo-Ryu Karate. You train in this martial art for a week and then sit down to evaluate what you are learning. The instructors at the dojo don't seem to know what they are doing. The techniques they are teaching you seem unnecessarily complicated. You don't think they would work in a real fight. You open your laptop and do some research on Bogo-Ryu karate. You can't find any information about it. You conclude that the whole martial art is bogus and confront your sensei about it. He admits that Bogo-Ryu Karate is something he just made up in order to make money, and that because he has never had any formal martial arts training, he is wholly unqualified to teach others martial arts.

In this situation, a revelation occurred to you. This revelation was that the martial art you were studying was bogus. This is not the type of revelation that is represented by process of being struck by lightning depicted in the Tower card because that represents a painful revelation. The revelation that occurred to you wasn't painful. You spent a week learning a bogus martial art, but one week isn't too big of a deal. You might be mad at the sensei for deceiving you, but you're mostly relieved to have caught on to his shenanigans before he could con you out of too much money or waste too much of your time. In fact, the week you spent undergoing this experience wasn't a complete waste of time because, while you didn't learn any real karate, you did learn something else. You learned that it's important to do some research on a martial arts instructor, his school, and the martial art he teaches before you begin studying from him.

Now let's imagine a different situation. You train in Bogo-Ryu Karate for thirty years. One day while walking through a dark alley a person twice as small as you jumps you and beats you up for fun. Although you are twice as big as your assailant, you don't stand a chance against him. Years of training have programmed you to fight using Bogo-Ryu techniques, and these techniques are wholly ineffective. You wake up in a hospital and realize you have wasted thirty years of your life practicing a completely ineffective martial art. This revelation is the kind of revelation depicted in the Tower card.

In the first situation, you objectively analyzed Bogo-Ryu and realized it was bogus. In the second situation, you did not objectively analyze Bogo-Ryu and therefore you never learned that it was bogus. Think back to Jake. Jake never objectively analyzed himself or he would have realized that he was more immature that the average toddler and a complete slave to his passions. In contrast, when we examine the lives of genuine adepts, living or dead, we find that they are extremely mature and that they have overcome the influence of their passions. This isn't to say they have no passions. However, instead of the influence of their passions, it is reason, conscience, intuition, and wisdom that dictate their actions and determine their choices. These people weren't born like that. Like all human beings, they were born immature in many ways. Like all human beings, they were born at least partially enslaved by the passions. They could have ended up like Jake, but they didn't because they did what Jake wouldn't do. They objectively analyzed themselves. In this way, they learned the ways in which they were immature and the ways in which they were a slave to their passions. Armed with this knowledge, they were able to take the steps necessary to become mature and to establish the elemental equilibrium that would free them from their passions and connect them with the wisdom of their higher selves.

You can study esotericism for thirty years and end up thinking you are enlightened or whatever. However, if for some reason you wake up one day and realize that you're actually just an incredibly immature brat, that revelation is going to hurt as much as if you'd been knocked off a tower by lightning.

The best way to avoid becoming extremely immature is to actively strive to become more mature. This process starts by eliminating from your being the various ways in which you are currently immature. However, in order to do that, you must learn the ways in which you are immature. If you are a Bardonist, then the next step after learning these ways is to write them down in your black soul mirror so you don't forget about them. In other words, the process of becoming more mature begins with objectively analyzing and reflecting upon yourself and your life to discover the ways in which you are immature. This is an example of the process known in magic as "introspection."

Now, some of you readers might be thinking "Isn't that obvious." It is. My point in writing all of this is two-fold. First, there are many people who are bad at seeing the obvious. Second, I want to set the stage for some of the topics I will discuss in later chapters of this book. Introspection is important. That's obvious. However, to get the most out of introspection, you should approach the process of introspection intelligently. Furthermore, you should arrange your life in such a way that facilitates the practice of productive and effective introspection. The manner in which to do this is worth discussing in detail, and I will do so at various points throughout this book, especially in Chapter 11.

Imagine a man who is extremely forgetful. However, he doesn't want to acknowledge the fact that he is extremely forgetful.

One day, he forgets to turn off the stove. His whole house burns down and, since the rest of his family was in the house, they perish because of his mistake. Now he can no longer deny that he is extremely forgetful. He woke up to this fact in a very painful manner when the lightning bolt struck in the form of his house burning down.

I have a less tragic example that illustrates the same principles. When I was in college I took a course in multi-variable calculus. I thought I had learned the material pretty well and therefore didn't feel the need to study too hard for the first exam. I ended up failing the first exam. My low score on the first exam was a lightning bolt that woke me up, in a very painful manner, to the fact that I wasn't as good at calculus as I thought I was, and that I did need to study more. There are many ways I could have woken up to this fact in a less painful manner. For example, if I had worked through some practice exams, I could have observed that I was having more difficulty with them than anticipated and in this way realized I wasn't as good as I thought I was and needed to study more.

We experience devastatingly painful revelations about ourselves when we hide from the truth until the day we are at last compelled to confront the truth in such a way that resistance is futile. Regardless of whether that day involves watching your house burn down or failing a test, it's not fun. We can avoid devastatingly painful revelations by willingly and actively seeking out the truth. When we do this, we assimilate the truth before it becomes too painful to swallow. The man whose house burned down could have objectively analyzed himself (introspected) and in this way he learned that he was extremely forgetful. From this understanding, he would have known to take measures to improve his memory. There would have been no need for Divine Providence to send a lightning bolt to blast him awake because he would have already woken up peacefully on his own.

If the truth ever becomes too painful to swallow, then we permanently shelter ourselves from it by entering a permanent state of denial. This permanent state of denial is a dark bubble that shields us from the lightning bolt. It prevents the lightning bolt from reaching us and waking us up.

I mentioned in my first book, *The Spirit of Magic* when someone is in this dark bubble, it is possible for a very skilled magician to send a powerful blessing to help them become free and wake up gently and peacefully. The fact of the matter is, even if someone has built such a dark bubble around themselves, there is still a part of them existing deep down inside that still wants to learn the truth, no matter how painful the experience of learning the truth will be. In fact, when you're a magician, Divine Providence sometimes sends people into your life who need help seeing the truth and tasks you with helping them to open their eyes. If you read a lot of Bill's (William Mistele) writings, you might get the impression that the service performed by magicians always involves using the powers of the Cosmic Alphabet to help establish world peace. That's not the case. Service can take many forms.

However, it's not my intent to give magical techniques, methods, or strategies you can use to bless these people in such a way that they peacefully realize and accept whatever truth they need to accept in order to grow and mature. My point is that you must take all the measures you can to prevent yourself from falling into such a state that you cannot face the truth and have even built a dark bubble around yourself to shield yourself from the lightning bolt Divine Providence sends as a last resort to wake you up.

I want to end this chapter with a discussion of the four powers of the sphinx. These are as follows—to know, to dare, to will, and to keep silence. They are often presented in this order, and for good reason. If you are to complete an endeavor, you must first know the things you need to know in order to succeed. Once you have obtained this knowledge, you can dare to begin the endeavor. Once you have dared to begin the endeavor, you can will yourself to see the endeavor through to the end. Let's consider the endeavor of becoming more mature. You need to know a lot of things before starting this endeavor. You need to know the ways in which you are not mature. The lightning bolt infuses you with this knowledge, but it does so in a way that is disorienting and disturbing. It is better to acquire this knowledge through gentler means. Seek knowledge of yourself before life hits you with it in the form of a lightning bolt. Or, to put it another way, open your eyes to the ways in which you are immature before Divine Providence is forced to send a lightning bolt to blast your eyes open. That is all.

Chapter 3: The Intent Key

In his article on the first key, Frater Acher describes three "keys" that are essential to successfully completing a magical ritual.[4] These three keys are intent, structure, and awareness.

While Frater Acher applies these keys to the process of completing a magical ritual, they can be applied to any difficult process or endeavor, such as becoming a magician. In this chapter, I want to discuss the first key—the Intent Key.

The idea behind the Intent Key is that in order to successfully complete a difficult endeavor such as a magical ritual or magical training, you need to have the intent to complete the endeavor. This may seem like common sense, yet there are many people who never complete their magical training despite intending to do so. Possessing the Intent Key that Frater Acher describes does not just mean you want to succeed or desire to succeed.

At the beginning of a ritual, it's customary in several traditions of magic to make a declaration of intent. For example, you might say something like "I declare this temple open with the intent of performing a ritual to evoke the spirit Bethor." However, saying you intend to perform a ritual to evoke Bethor does not mean you truly possess the Intent Key when it comes to the ritual to evoke Bethor. According to Frater Acher, if we wish to perform a ritual such as an evocation of Bethor, we must first have developed the intent to succeed, and "only then can we enter the temple and utter our will without having our subconscious and a busload of entities laughing back at us."

Similarly, if you wish to successfully become a magician, you must possess the Intent Key when it comes to your training. Otherwise, if you try to work through a magical training system such as the Bardon system, your subconscious and a busload of demons will laugh at you. According to Frater Acher, there are two variants of the Intent Key. I will call them "Full Intent" and "Unconditional Devotion."

So, what exactly is the Intent Key? Frater Acher describes two variants of the Intent Key in his article. I will call them "Full Intent" and "Unconditional Devotion."

To possess Full Intent in regards to an endeavor means you have "a coherent conscious and subconscious understanding" of all aspects of the endeavor.

To possess Unconditional Devotion in regards to an endeavor means you are fully committed to completing the endeavor regardless of what it will take.

Let's consider the endeavor of reading a book in a language you do not know. For examine, imagine that a person who doesn't know Spanish wants to read Alberto Laiseca's *Matando Enanos a Garrotazos*. As soon as he decides to do this, his subconscious and a busload of entities will laugh at him. They will say "This guy thinks he is going to read *Matando Enanos a Garrotazos*, but he doesn't know Spanish. Ha-ha!"

However, let's say that this guy has "a coherent conscious and subconscious understanding" of everything involved in the process of reading Laiseca's book. Now his subconscious and the busload of entities can't laugh at him. They know that he knows that he needs to learn Spanish in order to read the book. Since he knows this and has still decided to read the book, clearly he is willing to learn Spanish first. Because he possesses Full Intent in regards to the endeavor of reading Laiseca's book, he is not laughed at.

Now let's say this guy is Unconditionally Devoted to his endeavor to read Laiseca's book. In this case, his subconscious and the busload of demons can't laugh at him either. They'll say to themselves, "Wow, this guy is really devoted. He might not know yet that he has to learn Spanish in order to read the book, but when he does learn this, he'll clearly be willing to learn the language, after all, look how devoted to this endeavor he is!"

The principles illustrated in the above example of trying to read Laiseca's book also apply to the endeavor of becoming a magician. Pick any random Bardonist who has decided to work through IIH and I will bet my bottom dollar that his subconscious and a busload of entities are laughing at him. He may have decided to work through IIH, but he has no idea what that really entails. Thus, his decision is somewhat of a joke. Of course, if he has "a coherent conscious and subconscious understanding" of everything that magical training entails, then there is nothing funny about his decision. Or, if he possesses unconditional devotion to his training and is therefore willing to go through it regardless of what it entails, then there is likewise nothing funny about his decision. However, if he doesn't know what magical training entails, or doesn't possess unconditional devotion to his training, then his decision to undergo magical training is a joke.

Let's discuss the process of acquiring Full Intent in regards to your magical training. Again, this means you have "a coherent conscious and subconscious understanding" of everything involved in magical training. Very few Bardonists possess Full Intent in regards to their training because they think magical training consists only of practicing magical exercises to develop magical skills and abilities. To acquire Full Intent in regards to your training, you need a coherent conscious and subconscious understanding of the aspects of magical training besides practicing magical exercises to develop magical skills and abilities. The purpose of this book is to make you aware of those other aspects and to help you begin to develop a coherent conscious and subconscious understanding of them. As I stated in the introduction of this book, most of these other aspects center on the development of maturity.

A Facebook post by Bill about the Bardon system includes a conversation between two demons about a kid who has recently begun working through IIH. This conversation is reproduced below.

Demon #1: Hey. There is this really stupid kid who just bought Bardon's *Initiation into Hermetics*. No, actually he downloaded it for free from the internet. And he has decided to make it his life's calling and vocation.

Demon #2 (falling over laughing). I hope he also draws pentagrams in the air in four directions. That always is good for a laugh. I love magicians. They are so incredibly entertaining. Where else can you find such arrogance combined with raw inexperience?

Demon #1: What will you wager me that I can get him to stop his practice within two months?

Demon #2: I won't take that bet. But I will bet you that I can turn him into a Hari Krishna or a fundamentalist Christian within a year if he keeps practicing.

Demon #1: I won't take that bet. I still owe you for your getting the author of *A Dweller on Two Planets* to return to Christianity along with Charles Williams and T.S Elliot and Bob Dylan.

Demon #2: Child's play. Ha Ha Ha.

The two demons are laughing at the kid because he doesn't know what he is getting into. In other words, he does have "a coherent conscious and subconscious understanding" of everything involved in the process of working through IIH. In other words, he doesn't possess Full Intent in regards to his magical training. If you have a coherent conscious and subconscious understanding of everything involved in magical training, there will be no surprises as you work to become a magician. If you don't have any understanding of what is involved in magical training, you will constantly face surprises, and some of those surprises can freak you out so much that you run away from magic and opt to practice a safer and less weird form of spirituality such as those found in organized religion.

Near the end of his article on the first key, Frater Acher presents this saying by his first teacher—"Any successful rite is accomplished before it was even begun." Since we have translated this model from a version pertaining to magical operations to a version pertaining to magical training, we might translate this saying as follows —"Any successful endeavor to work through IIH was completed before it was even begun."

Chapter 4: Mature Speech

Preliminary Notes on Speech

Speech is two things:[5]

1. A reflection of a person's maturity level
2. A means through which a person can change his maturity level

Speech is a reflection of a person's maturity level, meaning that by observing the way someone speaks, you can assess how mature he is. For example, let's say that someone is always gossiping, lying, boasting, belittling others, and insulting others. Since he speaks immaturely, you can safely assume he is immature. Now, let's say that someone always speaks intelligently, compassionately, and respectfully. Since he speaks maturely, you can safely assume he is mature.

Speech is also a means through which a person can change his maturity level, meaning that by forcing yourself to speak maturely, you will eventually become mature. By forcing yourself to speak immaturely, you will eventually become immature. Needless to say, no one intentionally does that, but it still happens. Whenever immature people speak immaturely, this act of speech reinforces their immaturity. Thus, if you are an immature person who is constantly speaking immaturely, a wise thing to do would be to just shut up until you learn to speak maturely, and then try to speak maturely until one day you really are mature and therefore no longer need to "try" in order to speak maturely.

Covert and Overt Immature Speech

There are two forms of immature speech—covert and overt. Boasting is one type of immature speech. Everyone who has been a member of any online occult forum or group has seen this type of speech in its overt form numerous times. In such forums and groups, people are constantly boasting about how long they've been studying occultism, or what degree they are in this or that magical order, or how old their magical lineage is, or how many evocations they've performed, etc.

Covert boasting is another matter. Let's say that someone writes an article about IIH. It seems like this article was written to help students of Bardon's system understand the book, but if the real reason the author wrote the book was to show off his knowledge of IIH and imply that he is an expert on Bardon's system, then the article is an example of covert boasting.

Lying is another type of immature speech.[6] Overt lying is also something everyone is familiar with. If you say something that is just plain false and you know it's false, then you are overtly lying.

Covert lying is when you say something that is technically true, but you word it in a way that is misleading and meant to get others to believe something false. For example, let's say that you are envious of someone named Steve and want to ruin his reputation. You tell everyone that you saw him slap his wife. This makes everyone think he abuses his wife. In reality, you just saw him give his wife a high five. You were overtly lying because what you said is literally true, but you were covertly lying. Therefore, from a magical point of view, you were still lying.

Insulting people is another type of immature speech. Some people disguise insults as constructive criticism, however, insults disguised as constructive criticism are still insults, and therefore, an example of immature speech. Insults are designed to hurt people —to hurt their self-esteem, to hurt their feelings, to hurt their reputation, etc. Insults are destructive. Constructive criticism, on the other hand, is designed to help people build themselves up. They are complete opposites.

Additional Notes on Speech

At the end of *Magical Rituals of the Sanctum Regnum*, Eliphas Levi provides a number of esoteric maxims. Three of those maxims are as follows:

Every idle word is a fault.

An idle word is either without meaning or is of the nature of a lie.

He who is content with idle words is as if he were dead.

Before coming across IIH, I studied Levi's writings extensively. Coming across these maxims was my first introduction to the idea that regulating one's speech was an important part of magical training.

Shortly after I started training in Bardon's system, a number of incidents happened in my life that quickly taught me the importance of regulating my speech. In one instance, I was unfairly bad mouthing a coworker whom I didn't notice was standing right behind me. That was embarrassing. In another instance, I was making fun of a waitress at a restaurant. I was speaking in Chinese to my friend and assumed that the waitress didn't know Chinese. It turns out she did. That was embarrassing too. A number of similar incidents happened, all in a very short span of time. It was clear to me that the universe was trying to teach me a very important lesson —regulate my speech. In other words, don't gossip, don't lie for selfish reasons, don't belittle others, don't make fun of others, don't insult others, etc.

When it came to basic magical training, Bardon could only fit so much into one book. He puts all of the absolutely necessary information in his first book. Thus, his system is complete. However, he also leaves students of his system to figure out a lot of stuff by themselves. The importance of regulating your speech is one thing Bardon never explicitly wrote about, but expected his students to eventually learn.

In KTQ, Bardon teaches the art of creative speaking. Literal human speech is NOT the same as the divine art of creative speaking, however, they are analogous. IIH is not the be all and end all of magical training. It prepares you to learn and work with much higher and advanced forms of magic, including evocation and creative speaking.

Creative speaking is a powerful means to shape the world. The negative effects from its abuse can result in a lot of suffering for innocent people and a severe karmic backlash for the one who abuses this art. In order to protect the would-be abuser and his would-be victims, Divine Providence puts in place certain restrictions that prevent the immature from learning creative speaking. How those restrictions manifest themselves in the lives of specific aspiring magicians varies on a case by case basis.

Using literal human speech responsibly (or as I've previously put it, "regulating" it) shows Divine Providence that you can use the divine art of creative speaking responsibly. Since IIH is designed in part to prepare you to learn creative speaking, part of doing the work of IIH is learning to regulate your speech. In this way, when you complete Step 8 and are ready to move on to the work of KTQ, you will have learned how to speak responsibly, and therefore, Divine Providence knows you can be trusted to make use of creative speaking responsibly.

Another way of thinking about it is this. If you are a mature person, then you will speak like a mature person. Mature people don't gossip, lie for selfish reasons, belittle others, make fun of others, insult others, etc. Of course, they can point out the errors of others and offer constructive criticism, but this is never done in a way that is disrespectful or unnecessarily hurtful.

Thus, we have the following situation:

Inner state = immature

Outer manifestation (of inner state) = immature use of speech

One of the things you'll learn in your magical training is that self-transformation almost always works from the outside in. For example, let's say you don't have an elemental equilibrium but want to develop one. We end up with the following situation:

Inner state = elements within oneself are impure and unbalanced

Outer manifestation (of inner state) = one exhibits negative traits like irritability, laziness, stupidity, and dishonesty.

Can you establish an elemental equilibrium by using magical techniques to directly purify and balance the elements within you? Nope. You can't do that. Numerous modern magical systems make the mistake of thinking you can. They use various elemental correspondences (divine names, colors, symbols, regions of the body) in an attempt to force the elements constituting one's subtle bodies into a balanced and pure state. While this might seem logical at first, anyone with a solid understanding of the occult anatomy and karma will realize that it is a naïve and ineffective approach for establishing an elemental equilibrium. Again, as is often the case, you work from the outside in. In my second book (*The Elemental Equilibrium: Notes on the Foundation of Magical Adepthood*), I give a number of magical techniques for eliminating negative traits like irritability, laziness, stupidity, and dishonesty. By working on these outer manifestations, the inner state giving rise to these manifestations will change. The elements constituting your subtle bodies will go from an impure and unbalanced state to one of purity and balance, thus establishing an elemental equilibrium within yourself.

A similar principle is at work when it comes to regulating your speech. When you are immature, you speak immaturely. By forcing yourself to speak maturely, you slowly begin transforming your inner state so that it becomes more mature. "As without, so within."

Being Accountable

Levi writes the following in *The Magical Ritual of the Sanctum Regnum.*

"Be guarded in the words you speak. Speak not of God, unless you are illuminated. All the images which you create, whether of God or of other ideals, remain imprinted on that luminous medium—the astral light of the soul, and of the world and there is that Book of the Conscience which shall be opened and its records revealed in the Last Day."

This is, I believe, Levi's way of saying that you are accountable for everything you say, even if you don't think you are. The universe tried to teach me this lesson very early in my training. I already mentioned the two stories where I was saying negative things about people without realizing they were listening to me. Sometimes you don't think you will be held accountable for what you say about another person because they aren't listening so you can say whatever you want about them. That's never true. The astral light records everything and will hold you accountable for what you say. To become responsible is part of the process of becoming more mature, and part of being responsible is being responsible for the things we say.

Words are Like Swords

In Kenji Tokitsu's translation of Miyomoto Musashi's *Book of Five Rings*, he writes the following in the introduction.

"Like a sword, a word can wound or kill, but as long as one does not tough the blade, the sword is no more than a smooth piece of metal. Someone who knows the qualities of a sword does not play with it, and someone

who knows the nature of words does not play with them."

These are true words. Be careful what you say. I grew up with a sharp tongue and was always hurting people with it. As you can probably imagine, I wasn't able to make much progress in the work of IIH until I fixed that problem. Can you imagine someone who cannot even control his own mouth trying to control the elements? It is ridiculous, but that was me.

We don't give swords to immature people because they're either going to hurt themselves or hurt others with it. It's the same case with words. If you don't use them maturely, you're going to inflict a lot of unnecessary suffering upon others and upon yourself. Do yourself and the rest of the world a favor by learning to speak maturely.

Forming Your Speech Code

Some people might find it helpful to write their own code that provides guidelines when it comes to refraining from speaking immaturely. An example of a speech code is below:

1. Avoid making negative remarks about others unless it is absolutely necessary to do so.

2. If you ever do need to criticize someone, make sure to word the criticism in the least hurtful and most respectful way possible.

3. Don't talk about spirituality unless it is unavoidable. This means don't bring up spirituality, religion, etc. when conversing with others. If the subject of spirituality and religion does somehow end up getting brought up during a conversation, talk about these subjects as if you had no interest in these subjects.

4. If you do end up talking about spirituality with someone, do not mention anything related to magic or esotericism unless it is unavoidable. If the subjects of magic and esotericism do somehow end up coming up, talk about them as if you had no interest in them.

5. Do not make false or exaggerated statements.

The Speech Journal

It is a good idea to keep a speech journal as you endeavor to make mature speech a way of life. This is a journal in which you record all the times you speak immaturely. Each time you speak immaturely, pull out your smartphone and make a note of what you said. That way, at the end of the day, you can just look at your smartphone to see what to record in your journal. You don't have to reflect back on the day and try to remember all of the ways you spoke immaturely so you can record them. The speech journal will help you see how quickly you are becoming more mature, and whether there are any patterns in the way you speak immaturely.

A segment from my own speech journal is contained in the next chapter. There are several things to note.

First, note that I do not write in the journal every day. Some days, I don't speak immaturely in any way so there is nothing to record. Also, note that the entries either begin with "Today" or "On this day." If an entry begins with "Today," then that means the events described in that entry were recorded the same day they took place. If an entry begins with "On this day," that means I forgot to write in my speech journal on the day the events occurred and am recording them either the next day or at some later date. The date above each entry gives the date the events happened, which is not necessarily the date they were recorded because I was really forgetful back then and often neglected to record speech infractions.

Also, note that I reference the code given in the previous section several times. Like I said, having your own code is useful.

However, each person should have their own unique code. For example, I restrict myself from talking about general spirituality or religion. That's because whenever I talk about general spirituality or religion, I always end up referencing magical ideas and concepts. Thus, talking about general spirituality and religion inevitably leads me to end up talking about esotericism and magic. However, if that's not the case for you, you may feel no need to have a code that restricts you from talking about esotericism and general spirituality.

As one final note, I want to point out that I did not write down the times of the infractions, but after someone advised me to do this, I have begun doing so and think it is a beneficial practice. Thus, in your journal, I suggest that you not only record instances where you spoke immaturely during the day, but that you also note down what time during the day of the instance If you can't record the exact time, record the general time (early morning, around noon, late in the evening, etc.).

Chapter 5: An Excerpt from a Speech-Regulation Journal

5/27/06

Today when I was talking to Gary, I wasn't present-minded. Therefore, I wasn't actively paying attention to what I was saying and making a conscious effort to restrict my words. During this conversation, I criticized Greg, calling him disorganized. I should not have done this.

Before then, I was about to tell Gary that I snuck into Dave's office to eat lunch because the air conditioner in my office was broken. I told him that because I thought it would be funny if I had done it, but I didn't do it so that was a lie.

In the future, be always present-minded when talking. In this way, you can actively pay attention to what you are saying and make a conscious effort to restrict your words, so you don't say anything critical of others or immature and foolish.

Furthermore, don't lie. It goes against your values. Also, you risk getting caught.

5/29/06

Today while talking with Nick and Alexa, I said that Selena is great at answering questions without actually answering them. I shouldn't have said this. Also, I said that Selena didn't really answer my question, but she actually did. My own stupidity just prevented me from understanding her answer.

During the EGGC meeting, I made that joke about giving the new people a book on hardware and telling them to read it on their own time. I should not have done this.

6/1/06

On this day, I saw Andy briefly around 4:30. He told me he couldn't meet with me and asked me if I could meet later during the day. My response was excessively verbose. I should have answered more concisely.

6/3/06

Today when James said he didn't learn anything from the orientation, I agreed and said that they just wasted our time. I should avoid making critical or insulting remarks about other people.

During the taxi ride to the advising session, I remarked that the advising sessions really weren't that helpful and criticized the people who organized them and made us go do them.

While we were all introducing ourselves at the advising session, I said "Yes" when asked if I'd ever been to Spain. That was a lie. I just wanted to seem well-traveled.

6/8/06

Today I made two huge mistakes. I consciously brought up politics during a conversation when it was not necessary to, and I consciously brought up spirituality during a conversation when it was not necessary to.

I was conversing with Gary and he was talking about how narrow-minded some people can be. He remarked that the other day, he met someone who was so narrow-minded that it blew his mind. I said that I also knew of someone that narrow-minded and began talking about NN.[7]

During this same conversation, Gary mentioned that he used to do kung fu and wants to get back to it. We started talking about that, I brought up stuff like chi, meditation, and the Buddhist roots of some styles of kung fu. This led to a discussion of spirituality in general. During that discussion, I brought up concepts like the higher self and the Kabbalistic Tree of Life.

6/10/06

Today, while eating lunch together, Gary said he hadn't heard anything nice about Pete. I said there isn't anything nice to say about him. I shouldn't have said that because it's mean.

6/11/06

Today, when telling Dave about the trip to the GHP meeting, I exaggerated the shortness of the time I spent there. I did this because I thought it would be funny if we went there and almost immediately came back. Later, when telling Gary about the trip to the GHP meeting, I did the same thing.

Don't exaggerate. It is a form of dishonesty. An exaggerated statement is a lie, and comes with all the spiritual and practical dangers that surround lies.

6/13/06

Today while talking with Thomas, I brought up the subject of gaslighting. I didn't need to bring it up, and did it just to say something, and perhaps seem a bit interesting (in other words, seem like someone who has things to talk about). The reason I brought that subject up, out of all the subjects I could've brought up, is because I had just been reading an article about it so it was at the top of my mind. I shouldn't have brought the subject up because it is negative and I should avoid bringing up negative subjects unless it's necessary to do so.

6/14/06

Today when criticizing that essay, I could have been less harsh when explaining that it was disorganized, full of grammar errors, and difficult to understand. I think part of the reason I used unnecessarily harsh language is that part of me harbors resentment against her for how bigoted she can be. This resentment moved me to use unnecessarily harsh language. It's situations like this that are our greatest tests when it comes to regulating speech, but they can also lead to the greatest victories. Today I was not victorious. I should have worded my criticism of the essay in the least hurtful manner possible. I did not do this.

She was trying to become a better writer and I should have been happy that she respected my skills as a writer enough to ask me for help. I should have sought to support her instead of knock her down.

6/17/06

On this day Ashley saw me reading while sitting on the floor outside the lounge and asked me why I was studying there. I replied "I liked it here," but my tone was somewhat indignant. I used an indignant tone because I think of her as annoying, despite having no good reason to. She was just trying to be friendly. I should have given a more friendly response in a more friendly tone.

6/20/06

Today while talking with Thomas, I told him that my roommate is extremely talkative and that this makes him annoying to the point where I can't stand him. I shouldn't have said this because my code says to avoid making critical remarks unless it is necessary to do so. Furthermore, it's an exaggeration anyway.

7/5/06

Today while talking to Gary, I said that Miranda is always late. While that's true, I shouldn't have said it because it's an unnecessary critical remark.

7/10/06

Today while talking about Star Wars with Dave, I brought up spirituality again. I mentioned how the "Force" is similar to both the western idea of God and the Chinese concept of chi. This led to a long discussion about both God and chi, in which I ended up bringing up esoteric concepts like the astral plane and the astral body. That was a fail, but at least Dave already knew I was interested in esotericism.

7/17/06

Today during the EGGC meeting, I told Andrew "Print out three copies of the article." I should have said something like "Could you print out three copies of the article please" or "Do you think it would be a good idea to print out copies of the article?" I wanted to seem like the kind of person with a commanding or in-charge personality to impress him, but I think I came off as rude. Don't try to impress people by ordering people around. Be polite. It is more important to be compassionate than to come across as macho.

7/18/06

Today I mentioned and showed Dave the book about Kabbalah I checked out from the library as part of a joke. I told him he could read it if he ever got bored, knowing he would never do that. I shouldn't have done that. While Dave does know I am interested in esotericism, I should stop reminding him. I already have a bad track record when it comes to the fourth power of the sphinx. I need to take measures to repair the damage I have done to myself and my spiritual evolution from not keeping silence.

7/23/06

Today all of the things I said out of anger, frustration, or exasperation should either not have been said or should have been worded or spoken in a more kind, polite, or pleasant manner. See anger journal for specific details.

I told an anecdote to Dave about a guy I knew who scanned the PC papers to study at home. Parts of the anecdote were embellished to make it seem more incredible and a better story.

7/28/06

Today I messed up pretty badly. While conversing with Dave about the XXX episode "XXX," I mentioned that I believe in souls. I also began talking about the aspect of my life that is interacting with people interested in magic, occultism, esotericism, and New Age spirituality. I mentioned things like the subtle bodies, astrology, and past life regression.

Dave already knew I was into this stuff; however I still should not have brought it up. I believe it started when I mentioned that I believe in souls. Since there was nothing explicitly magical about that, I thought this was fine, but somehow this lead to a discussion of subtle bodies, and then of how astrological forces supposedly shape one's subtle bodies, and then of other occult topics.

I forgot that my code says, "I should not bring up spiritual subjects in general and should avoid conversations about spiritual subjects." While souls are not explicitly magical, they do fall under the category of spirituality, so I should not have mentioned them.

7/29/06

Today when riding with Gary back from the advising session, I made some negative comments about the chances of the attempt to teach all of the new people everything they need to know about Java in two weeks. While nothing I said was super offensive or insulting or mean, it was uncomfortably close to the line. I also said "Don't tell Andrew I'm saying this," which I shouldn't have said, because it makes what I was saying seem worse than it actually was.

After returning to the office, I started gossiping with Dave about Mike. At some point Mike returned while Dave and I were still conversing, but by that time the topic of our conversation had changed to something completely different. This is a good reminder that even when you think you are safe, you might not be. Avoid criticizing or gossiping about people. When criticizing people, use the least harsh wording possible. Speak the truth.

7/1/06

Today when Nick invited me to the party and asked me if I was coming, I said I didn't want to go, but the way in which I said that was unnecessarily snarky.

7/6/06

Today Dave began talking to me about a court case that was a major win for those in favor of same-sex marriage. Since a lot of opposition to same-sex marriage comes from those who are religious, we started talking about religion. The Bible was brought up, and I started talking about how in Kabbalah there are different levels of interpretation of the Bible, so often the real meaning of a passage is not the same as the literal meaning of the passage. I shouldn't have brought up Kabbalah.

7/10/06

Today I started ranting to Dave about the rude guy at the meeting. The guy was definitely rude, but I should avoid making critical remarks unless they serve some productive purpose.

Chapter 6: Malkuth

Bill's (William Mistele) extended essay on the *Ten Sephiroth of the Tree of Life,* contains a chapter for each sephiroth. Each sephirah's chapter contains several exercises for understanding the mysteries and lessons pertaining to that sephirah.

The first two exercises for Malkuth are as follows:

1. Carefully observe your routines and seize opportunities as they occur to improve on what you are doing.
2. Turn your life into a story worth telling.

These are genuinely magical exercises, and are interwoven with the work of IIH. Therefore, I want to discuss them a bit.

When I contemplate the first exercise, I am reminded of alchemy. Just as an alchemist continually refines a metal to improve it, you continually refine the way you do anything, whether it is conversing with others, cooking, driving, playing with your kids, or eating. By constantly refining the way you do these things, you improve the way you do these things until you can do them almost perfectly.

Another thing I am reminded of is a quote by Paul Foster Case from a book he wrote that discusses using magical techniques to improve yourself, improve your life, and achieve your goals. The quote is as follows.

> *"Don't waste a moment's time trying to think up some high and lofty objective, far ahead in life. Life is not lived by years. It is an affair of days, hours—minutes even. Today's activities determine the fulfillment of tomorrow's ideals."*

I think the spirit of this quote aligns well with the spirit of the two Malkuth exercises given by Bill. With the first exercise, you're not trying to become an adept, or become enlightened, or accomplish some other high and lofty objective. You're just trying to improve the way you do the things you do in your ordinary day to day life. This really is an affair of minutes. You might cook for a few minutes, or drive for a few minutes, or converse with someone for a few minutes. A lot of the time, it is actually an affair of seconds. Washing your hands doesn't take several minutes. Yet, a magician can always improve the way he washes his hands by becoming better and better at using the magnetic fluid in the water to absorb away his negative traits and carry them down the drain.

For the student of magic, the ideal of tomorrow is to be a person than he is today. Whether this ideal comes to pass tomorrow is, as Case says, entirely dependent on the activities he does today. It's not dependent on any one particular activity. Every activity you do today determines whether you will be a better person tomorrow. For this reason, at any moment in time, it's important to be focused on whatever you are doing so you can consciously strive to do your best and take mental notes on what you can do to improve. For example, let's say you are practicing a kata. If you aren't present-minded, your movements will be sloppy. Practicing the kata in a sloppy manner may make you worse, rather than better. If you practice the kata while present-minded, then you consciously strive to do the best that you can do. In this way, you will truly improve. This also gives you the opportunity to make mental notes about other things you can do to improve. For example, you might notice that you are not good at remaining in zenkutsu dachi. With this knowledge, you might decide to do some stance training later. However, if you are absent-minded instead of present-minded when you practice the kata, you will not notice these things.

In summary, in order to improve the way you do something —cooking, karate, conversing, flirting, etc—you need to try your best while doing it. In order to try your best, you have to be focused. This is why present-mindedness is so important, and why I devote a whole chapter to the subject of present-mindedness later in this book.

Besides the importance of present-mindedness, another thing I notice is that in order to improve the way you do things, it is often necessary to transform your personality in some way. For example, let's say you are a college student who is bad at taking exams. You will probably do better if you develop the quality of intelligence while eliminating the quality of stupidity from yourself. This can be done with the "Six-Pronged Attack[8]," which I discuss in great detail in my second book (*The Elemental Equilibrium: Notes on the Foundation of Magical Adepthood.*)

Yet another thing I notice is that journaling can be a powerful asset to this exercise for some people, including myself. For journaling to be helpful, it needs to be approached in the right way. What the right way is will be different for different people. I like to spend an hour once a week writing in my journal. I document the all the things I like about the way I lived during the previous week, as well as all the ways I am disappointed in how I lived during the previous week. I might note down, for example, that I did a good job staying present-minded, but wasted a lot more time on social media than I wish I had. I'll also write down plans and suggestions for the upcoming week so that it will be better than the previous week in regards to the way I live and use my time. The insights I gain from journaling like this go a long way in helping me improve the way I do the things I do.

Having discussed the first Malkuth exercise Bill gives, let's discuss the second one. I find this exercise particularly interesting. Crowley theorized that the wand, sword, cup, and pentacle of the magicians evolved from the stylus, ink holder, sharpening blade, and paperweight of the first scribes. Just as a scribe uses those instruments to write a story, the magician uses those same tools to write out his destiny. The wand represents the airy aspect of a magician once it has been refined and developed. In other words, to possess a magical wand means that you have acquired positive airy traits like intelligence and open-mindedness, and eliminated from yourself all negative airy traits like absent-mindedness and shyness. Similarly, the sword, cup, and pentacle represent the fiery, water, and earthy aspects of the magician once they have been refined and developed.

There are several ways of attributing the four elements to the Sephiroth of the Tree of Life. One popular way is to attribute air to

Tiphereth, fire to Geburah, water to Chesed, and earth to Malkuth. Another possible way is to place all four elements in Malkuth. This method is probably the most relevant method for Bardonists who use Qabalah as a tool in their training. Malkuth in the macrocosm is the Earthzone, and the four elemental regions where the sylphs, salamanders, undines, and gnomes dwell are all contained within the Earthzone. Thus, it is fitting that a Malkuth exercise should involve establishing an elemental equilibrium; that is to say, acquiring the true wand, sword, cup, and pentacle.

Of course, having a stylus, sharpening blade, ink holder, and papyrus is not enough to begin writing a beautiful, wonderful, and interesting story. You also need to brainstorm ideas and come up with a plot for your story. Similarly, you need to brainstorm and come up with ways to make your life interesting so that when you die, people will love to hear the story of your life. One way to do this is to make a bucket list. Many example bucket lists can be found on the internet. From there, you just need to prioritize the items on the list and make plans for fulfilling them. Later on in your training, after you have completed Step 8 of IIH, you will find that there are numerous spirits in the Earthzone and in the planetary spheres who can give you support and guidance as you carry out those plans. That said, you shouldn't wait until you have completed IIH before beginning to carry out your plans. Do that as soon as possible.

Because the four elements pertain to Malkuth, and because the four elements are a major theme in IIH, it's clear there is some kind of profound connection between IIH and Malkuth. For this reason, one might come to the conclusion that these two exercises presented by Bill are somehow woven into the work of IIH. This conclusion is correct. Of course Bardon never explicitly describes either of these exercises in the text of the book, but when I reflect upon the time I spent working through IIH, it becomes apparent to me that I was doing these two exercises all along.

Bill also writes the following in the Malkuth chapter of his extended essay.

> *"Life is short. Make every effort not to get bogged down."*

According to Bill, the two exercises he gives are specifically designed to help you do just that—not get bogged down in life. Your magical training is an aspect of your life and should be well-integrated with the other aspects of your life. Thus, we might consider not getting bogged down in your magical training to be a part of not getting bogged down in life. I want to discuss this part of the practice a bit.

Many people get bogged down in their training. You see this in instances where people spend several years on Step 1. There are multiple things these people can get bogged down in. A lot of them get bogged down in their immaturity. Again, the way Bardon wrote IIH makes it seem like magical training is just about mastering exercise after exercise. Although, I've stated several times already that this is not the case, numerous people continue to believe it is. Since they are unaware that one's maturity affects one's rate of magical advancement, they never realize they are bogged down in their immaturity. They believe that the solution to their problem is to practice the exercises of IIH for several hours a day. This a really bad idea, and often leads to what is known as "magical burnout." If you are bogged down in your own immaturity, the best solution to your dilemma is to work strategically and persistently towards becoming more mature. This will remove the invisible walls you are butting your head against when you practice magical exercises and find yourself unable to advance, despite putting many hours into practicing those exercises.

Bill also includes a section on "well-being" in the Malkuth chapter. I think it's important to discuss well-being in regards to magical training; in particular Step 1, because well-being is exactly what many beginning Bardonists don't feel. Instead, they feel uncertain about whether they have what it takes to complete their training. They feel anxious about finding time each day to practice. They feel despair because the magical path seems so difficult. They feel worried about how they can juggle their magical training with their other interests and activities. This mixture of negative feelings isn't great. Until you've developed a sense of well-being, you won't make any significant progress in your training. The reason is that in order to make lasting progress, your magical training needs to be well-integrated into your life and in harmony with all other parts of your life. If this is the case, your magical training should not have a negative impact on your sense of well-being. Rather, it should enhance your sense of well-being because there are many positive benefits to be gained from magical training, assuming it is approached in the right way.

Bill also writes the following about gnomes in the Malkuth chapter:

> *"Gnomes are those beings who are most at home in the physical world. They consider matter itself to be spiritual and they are continuously seeking to shape and to transform it, raising its vibration and adding soul and mind to its nature. Gnomes possess a quiet ecstasy. Whatever they are working at, they are doing it with all of their heart. For gnomes, a unit of time is measured in terms of when they began and then completed a project. Time is defined from within."*

In magical training, you work to develop all four elements within yourself. Thus, you possess the positive traits of a gnome, a sylph, an undine, and a salamander. It is developing the gnome part of yourself and learning to approach your tasks like a gnome that I want to discuss now.

Gnomes continually work to refine and transform matter. When you have completed your magical training, you are a different person than before. You have an elemental equilibrium. You possess certain magical skills and abilities. You have become noble and righteous. In the same way that a gnome refines and transforms matter, you have refined and transformed yourself. Some people think that a "fiery" approach to working through IIH is the best. Through willpower, you blast through all obstacles in your path. Other people think that an "airy" approach to working through IIH is the best. Through intelligent reasoning and logic, you come up with an excellent plan to overcome any obstacle and then put that plan into action. Other people think a "watery" approach to working through IIH is the best. Any time you come across an obstacle preventing you from advancing, you find a way to adapt and flow around the obstacle. In truth, the ideal approach to IIH has the nature of all four elements. I feel that the earth/gnome aspect of most people's approach to working through IIH is the weakest, and this is why their progress is slow. Consider, for example, that patience is a virtue of the earth element. Many people impatiently try to rush through IIH as fast as they can. Gnomes don't rush through their work. They work steadily and persistently at the pace most comfortable with them. Since "time is defined from within," they feel to no need to hurry.

Try to approach all aspects of your magical training more like a gnome and see what happens. Refine your ability to practice conscious breathing, conscious eating, and magical washing the way a gnome refines matter. Refine your ability to concentrate, accumulate energy, and exteriorize your subtle bodies the way a gnome refines matter. Refine your ability to see, hear, and feel astral-mental phenomena the way a gnome refines matter. Refine yourself the way a gnome refines matter. Document what happens when you do this. You will be surprised at what the patience and thoroughness of a gnome can help you accomplish.

Chapter 7: Present-Mindedness

In the previous chapter, I discussed two practices Bill gives to help aspiring magicians master the lesson of Malkuth. One of those practices is as follows.

> *"Carefully observe your routines and seize opportunities as they occur to improve on what you are doing."*

In my discussion of this practice, I mentioned that it was necessary to be constantly present-minded in order to do it. For this reason, in this chapter, I wish to provide a few musings on the present-mindedness exercises in a hope that they will help you understand this exercise better and master it more easily.

A New Look At the Second Mental Exercise of Step 1

There are four mental exercises in Step 1. Historically, the second and third exercises have always been viewed as essentially the same exercise. Thus, according to Rawn, although there are four exercises, there are only three types of exercises. In *A Bardon Companion*, he writes the following:

> *"The second type of meditation is titled "Thought Discipline" and has two phases of practice. The first phase is enacted in day-to-day life and involves disciplining your thoughts so that they pertain only to the task at hand. For example, if you're driving to work, you practice the shunning of thoughts that have nothing to do with the act of driving. The second phase of the practice is performed as a normal meditation (i.e., sitting with your eyes closed). Here, one chooses a single thought and shuns the intrusion of all other thoughts. It is best, in this instance, to begin with a*

simple, captivating thought. Each time your mind wanders, bring it firmly back to the chosen thought."

The first mental exercise is about awareness. The second and third mental exercises are usually both seen as concentration exercises. The fourth mental exercise is about stilling and emptying your mind.

In the second mental exercise, you are concentrating on what you are doing in the present-moment.

In the third mental exercise, you are concentrating on a specific thought. It doesn't matter what you are concentrating on; you're still concentrating, and thus, the same mental skill is being trained in both exercises.

Recently, after reflecting back on my own experience working thought Step 1, I've come to a different understanding of the second mental exercise.

The first exercise is about awareness; after all, you are being aware of your mind and all the thoughts passing through it.

The third exercise is about concentration; after all, you are concentrating on a specific thought. I don't think the second exercise is just meant to be a concentration exercise; I think the second exercise is supposed to bridge the gap between awareness and concentration. When you begin working on the second exercise, it is an awareness exercise. Slowly, over weeks of practice, it transforms into a concentration exercise.

So when you first start working on the second mental exercise, don't try to concentrate on what you are doing in the present moment. Instead, just try to remain aware of what you are doing in the present moment. Slowly, over time, your awareness of what you are doing in the present moment will transform into a concentration on what you are doing in the present moment. This transformation will happen on its own. In this way, you gradually go from learning to be aware to learning to concentrate. At this point, you can begin working on the formal concentration exercise, which is the third exercise.

By coming to a better understanding of the second mental exercise after reflecting on the exercise and my own experience working with it, I have come to understand both awareness and concentration better; after all, the second mental exercise is the bridge between awareness and concentration. I now realize that in many ways, awareness and concentration are at two ends of a sliding scale. Awareness is just concentrating on something big. Concentration is just being aware of something small. Think about it. In the first exercise (awareness), you are concentrating on your whole mind, which is something big. In the third exercise (concentration), you are allowing yourself to only be aware of one thought, which is something small. This is why the second mental exercise can be seen as either an awareness exercise or a concentration exercise. I think the reason a lot of people have trouble with this exercise is that they approach it as a concentration exercise right from the start when it is easier to approach it as an awareness exercise.

A New Approach to Learning Thought-Awareness

The first mental exercise is usually called "thought-observation," but in this section I am going to call it "thought-awareness," which I believe to be a better name for the exercise.

The second mental exercise is about being aware. I discussed this in the previous section. Consider this hypothetical approach to learning the first mental exercise.

You start off practicing the second mental exercise. You learn to be continually aware. Normally, there is a lot going on in the external world. Thus, your external surroundings and the physical actions you do as you interact with your external surroundings occupy most of your awareness. In any case, you continue to remain aware until you are proficient in being aware.

Then, one day, you sit down in a chair in an empty quiet room. You continue to do the second mental exercise. In other words, you continue to remain aware while sitting still in the chair. However, since you are sitting in any empty quiet room, there is not much going on in the external world, and you aren't doing much physically. Thus, the external world and your physical actions occupy only a small part of your awareness. Your inner environment—in particular your thoughts—occupy most of your awareness. Congratulations, you are now practicing the first mental exercise.

In this approach, you start off by becoming proficient in the second mental exercise, then you use that exercise to transition into doing the first mental exercise. The first and second exercises are both awareness exercises. Since they are essentially the same exercise, if you are proficient in the second exercise, it should be easy to become proficient in the first exercise.

The Secret Key to the Second Step 1 Mental Exercise

When people have a lot of difficulty with an exercise, they sometimes wonder if there is some secret that will make the exercise a lot easier.

For the second mental exercise, the answer is actually yes. It's that you can flush thoughts out of your mind with your breath. If you're at home and trying to be aware of/focus on your home life and what you are presently doing but work-related thoughts fill your mind and wrestle it away from what you are presently doing, just breathe the thoughts out.[9]

The Two Catalysts of my Mental Development

The rate of my mental development increased drastically thanks to two practices/tricks I learned and used regularly.

The first trick is the one I just mentioned in the previous section—that of using your breath to flush unwanted thoughts from your mind. This helped me greatly with the present-mindedness exercise of Step 1. Before, whenever my mind was filled with trivial thoughts, it took a lot of effort for me to fight the thoughts and suppress them. This strained my mind and was very frustrating. Once I learned I could just breathe out the thoughts, boy did my life become much easier. For example, let's say that I had just watched a movie and wanted to do some gardening, but I couldn't focus on my gardening because thoughts of the movie I just watched filled my mind. I could just breathe out the thoughts. Once my mind was empty, I could let gardening occupy it. In this way, I'd be successful in practicing the second mental exercise of being aware of what I was doing.

The second trick is to trace back the line of your thoughts once you become distracted. Many times, if we are practicing present-mindedness and realize we have started daydreaming or thinking about other things, we immediately turn our attention back to the present moment. Similarly, if we are practicing the third mental exercise of Step 1 and realize we are thinking about something other than the thought we were supposed to be concentrating on, we immediately turn our attention back to the thought we were supposed to be concentrating on. Instead of doing this, trace back the train of your thoughts from the point of departure from what you were supposed to be focusing on.

Consider the following hypothetical example. Let's say that I am taking a walk and trying to remain present-minded throughout the walk. Suddenly, in the middle of the walk, I realize that I am thinking about the movie IP Man 3, and therefore, am obviously not present-minded. Instead of turning my attention back to the present-moment, I trace the train of my thoughts back. Before I was thinking about IP Man 3 in general, I was thinking about a specific scene where IP Man (temporarily blinded) uses his hearing to evade Cheung Tin Chi's attacks and defeat him. Before I was thinking about that scene, I was thinking about a scene in Rogue One where Chirrut Îmwe (who is blind) uses his hearing to sense the location of the clone troopers and defeat them in battle. I thought of this scene because I heard the sound of a dog behind me. I didn't see the dog because I was facing in the other direction, but I knew it was behind me because I heard it.

So now I know that realizing a dog was behind me after hearing it reminded me of the scene in Rogue One where Chirrut Îmwe uses his hearing to sense the position of the clone troopers. Because Donnie Yen plays Chirrut Îmwe as well as IP Man, this reminded me of the scene in IP Man 3 where IP Man uses his hearing to evade Cheung Tin Chi's attacks. This is why I was thinking about IP Man 3 in the middle of my walk. Having followed my train of thoughts back to the moment where they departed from the present moment, I can resume focusing on the present moment.

Learning these two tricks and using the first one to expel unwanted thoughts instead of fighting them with willpower and using the second one whenever I became distracted greatly accelerated my mental development.

A Brief Note Regarding Rawn's Explanation of Present-Mindedness

In the second edition of ABC, Rawn writes that the second mental exercise of Step 1 involves "focusing your attention upon what you are physically doing." The problem with this explanation can be seen in the following situation.

Let's say that you wish to plan out your day tomorrow. This is a great way to stay organized and productive. Thus, you sit down in a chair and begin thinking about what you will do tomorrow and what time during the day you will do it.

The thing is, if you are thinking about what you are doing tomorrow, then you are not thinking about what you are physically doing in the present. You're sitting in a chair. As a student of Bardon's system, you should be constantly present-minded. If you go by Rawn's description of present-mindedness, you should focus your attention on sitting in the chair; however, this would prevent you from thinking about the next day so you can plan it out.

Sometimes we need to think about the future so we can plan it out. Sometimes, we need to reflect on the past so we can learn from our prior experiences.

I would define the present-minded exercise as centering your awareness on what you are doing in the present moment. Now, what you are doing could be physical (cooking, driving, etc). It could also be mental (calculating, reflecting, contemplating, analyzing, planning, etc). Rawn seems to assume that whatever you are doing is physical. That's not always the case.

So whatever you are doing, whether it is physical or mental (or emotional), just center/focus your attention on that.

The Biggest Misconception about the Present-Mindedness Exercise

If I had to explain the present-mindedness exercise, I would say "center your attention/awareness on what you are presently doing." In his commentary, Rawn says "focus your attention/awareness on what you are presently doing." These are more or less the same idea expressed in different wording. I want to point out something very important, however. Neither of us says "restrict your attention/awareness to what you are presently doing." That is not the present-mindedness exercise. A lot of people think it is, and this is the biggest misconception about this exercise. To center your attention on something is not to restrict your attention to it.

I'm going to use an analogy here. There are two types of vision—central vision and peripheral vision. If you are looking at something, it is in your central vision. However, there might be other stuff in your peripheral vision. Generally, however, you ignore what is in your peripheral vision and focus on what is in your central vision. When you look at an object in this way, your vision is centered on that object. Restricting your vision to that object would involve developing tunnel vision and then looking at it.

Think of your awareness as being composed of a "central awareness" and a "peripheral awareness." Whatever you are presently doing is in your central awareness, but there might be other stuff in your peripheral awareness. You don't have to have a "tunnel awareness" that encompasses just what you are doing in the present moment.

Centering your awareness on what you are presently doing isn't that hard. Restricting your awareness to what you are presently doing is hard and can cause a lot of mental strain, but that's not the exercise.

Now, no analogy is perfect. When you look at something using central vision and ignore the stuff in your peripheral vision, the stuff in your peripheral vision doesn't go away. However, when you focus your central awareness on something and ignore everything in your peripheral awareness, then often, whatever is in your peripheral awareness goes away. In this way, whatever you center your awareness on ends up occupying the entirety of your awareness anyway. If you want what you are presently doing to fill up the entirety of your awareness, this is the way to go. Trying to restrict you awareness to what you are presently doing right from the start will give you a headache.

So, to recap, when you do the present-mindedness exercise, don't try to restrict your awareness to the present. Center your awareness on the present. Then ignore what's in your peripheral awareness. What's in your peripheral awareness will eventually fade away. When this happens, the present will occupy the entirety of your awareness.

A String of Beads

Think of your magical training as a string of beads. Blue beads are mental exercises. Green beads are astral exercises. Yellow beads are physical exercises. Each time a bead appears on the string, you are practicing an exercise.

You don't practice magical exercises constantly. While that is what people obsessed with magic do, it's not what people serious about magic do. So, there's going to be a blue bead, a green bead, and a yellow bead next to each other. This set of three beads represents the daily practice session for one day. Then, there's going to be a gap, and then another set of three beads for next day's daily practice session.

However, there is a string that runs through all of the beads and connects them. This string is present-mindedness. While you are practicing your magical exercises, you are present-minded. When you are not practicing your magical exercises, you are also present-minded. Present-mindedness runs through your daily practice sessions and connects them.

A Note

In the next section, I describe an exercise that will greatly help you develop the quality of present-mindedness. Before I describe the exercise, I want to make a quick note. If you are addicted to daydreaming, then get rid of that negative trait first before practicing this exercise. The gist of present-mindedness training is this. Normally, you are not present-minded. You are absent-minded, or thinking about the past, or worrying about the future, or daydreaming. Each time you become present-minded, you try to remain present-minded for as long as you can before you slip into a distracted mental state. When you are addicted to daydreaming, then each time you become present-minded, instead of trying to remain present-minded, you willfully leave your present-minded state and start daydreaming instead because you're addicted to it. You don't bother trying to remain present-minded because daydreaming is fun and you would rather do that than be present-minded. Present-mindedness training is all about taking advantage of the brief moments when you are present-minded and trying to extend the length of those moments until they last indefinitely. If a negative trait, such as an addiction to daydreaming, makes you unwilling to take advantage of those moments, you will never succeed in present-mindedness training.

An Exercise for Present-Mindedness

Buy a notebook. Write the following in the notebook three times a day:

> *"Be present-minded. Always be aware. Every moment, focus on what you are doing. Center your attention on whatever your current task is. Be present-minded. Be present-minded. Be present-minded."*

One option is to write it shortly after every meal. In other words, shortly after eating breakfast, you'd pull out your notebook and write the imperative to yourself down. You'd then do the same immediately after lunch and dinner. Feel free to modify the written imperative to yourself however you want.[10]

Constant VOM

When you sit down to practice thought-observation/thought-awareness for ten minutes as Bardon has you doing in Step 1, you'll probably notice that your mind has quite a few thoughts at first. However, the longer you sit and observe your thoughts, the fewer thoughts there are. Note that you aren't intentionally trying to still or empty your mind. You're just observing it. However, the process of calmly and objectively observing your mind in a detached manner causes it to gradually become stiller and emptier. This is why when your timer finally goes off indicating that ten minutes are up, your mind is a lot stiller and emptier than it was when you began observing your thoughts.

So, in other words, the longer you practice thought-awareness, the emptier your mind gets. When you are present-minded, you are aware. This means that you are aware of the contents of your mind. Of course, you're also aware of the external world around you, but that's beside the point. To be present-minded is to be aware. Part of your awareness is always surrounding your mind and its contents (thoughts). Therefore, when you practice present-mindedness, you're also practicing thought-awareness. To be constantly present-minded is to be constantly practicing thought-awareness. Since your mind grows stiller and emptier the longer you observe it, constant present-mindedness leads to a constantly still and clear mind.

In Step 1, you attain a certain mastery over VOM. As you progress in your training, you need to deepen this mastery. The key to doing that is to stay constantly present-minded.

Chapter 8: Notes on Self-Transformation

"Man, and by man I do not mean either fools or profane people, man is worth whatever he believes himself to be worth. He can do whatever he believes himself capable of doing. He does whatever he really desires to do. He may at length become all that he wills to be."

~Eliphas Levi

The process of becoming more mature involves self-transformation. We must eliminate from ourselves the traits that make us immature (pettiness, arrogance, susceptibility to flattery, rudeness, etc.) and develop the traits that make a person mature (compassion, humbleness, responsibility, open-mindedness, etc.). My second book, *The Elemental Equilibrium*, was all about self-transformation and contains everything you need to know to shape yourself into a mature and balanced individual. That said, it certainly doesn't contain everything there is to know about self-transformation.

In this chapter, I want to discuss three subjects related to self-transformation that I didn't discuss in depth in *The Elemental Equilibrium: Notes on Magical Adepthood*. These are the motives of self-transformation, the types of control involved in self-transformation, and the so-called microscopic techniques of self-transformation.

The Motives of Self-transformation

There are many possible reasons a person could want to transform himself. Some of these reasons are listed below:

The Desire to Improve the World

A desire to improve the world can motivate you to transform yourself for the better. When you transform yourself for the better, you develop positive qualities such as organization, intelligence, persistence, and confidence. These positive qualities will make you more successful in any of your endeavors, including your endeavors to improve the world.

If you're the principal of a school, the decisions you make will affect the education of the students who attend your school. Making wise decisions will result in those students having a good education. Making unwise decisions will result in those students having a bad education. Therefore, developing wisdom will help you improve the world because you are improving the lives of your students and empowering them with a solid education.

If you're a scientist trying to develop biodegradable plastics or a civil engineer designing a skyscraper in such a way that it uses as much solar energy as possible, being intelligent will help you accomplish your task. Therefore, you would do well to use the Six-Pronged Attack to develop intelligence.

To improve the world is to change the world. To change something, you need power. Transforming yourself for the better in Step 2 puts you in a position to begin developing magical power in the later steps of IIH. Without an elemental equilibrium, one cannot acquire genuine magical power.

The Desire to be Liked by Others

Some people see a desire to be liked by others as a form of weakness. I don't. Of course, you shouldn't compromise your values, your integrity, or your dignity just to earn the approval of others, but at the same time, it's only natural to want to be liked. Furthermore, striving to be liked is an intelligent thing to do. Life is easier when people like you. Your boss will be more likely to give you a promotion if he likes you. Your current love interest will be more likely to agree to a date with you if she likes you. People will be more willing to do you favors if they like you.

To become liked by others, you need to transform yourself into a likable person. This often involves developing traits like compassion, charisma, a good sense of humor, intelligence, etc. It also involves eliminating the traits that make you unlikable (greed, rudeness, impatience, etc.).

The Desire to Improve the Lives of Your Family

I was on Reddit once and came across an anecdote about a guy who was addicted to heroin. The person relating this anecdote was closely related to the heroin addict. He ended the anecdote with this statement—"Don't become addicted to heroin. You'll wreck your own life, as well as the lives of everyone around you."

The writer of the anecdote detailed all of the ways everyone in the addict's life suffered because of the addict's addiction. Reading this anecdote reminded me of an important fact. You're not the only one who suffers because of your negative traits. Oftentimes, those around you suffer too. If you're careless, you might think that only affects you; however, if your carelessness causes you to accidentally leave the stove on when you go out and the house burns down, your whole family now has nowhere to live.

Because of this, the desire to improve the lives of your family and loved ones is another source of motivation when it comes to the work of self-transformation. As another example, if you are a mean asshole, your spouse and your kids will probably hate living with you. The quality of their lives will be low. Learning to be compassionate and considerate will improve their lives.

When you are a parent, you will face many problems. Let's say your kid spends all day playing video games. You want him to take up a productive hobby that is conducive towards good health (like a sport), but he is lazy so you will have a hard time convincing him. That's a problem. Or, let's say that your kid is doing badly in school despite trying his best. That's another problem. Or, let's say your kid is being bullied at school. That's yet another problem. You encounter problems all the time. How good you are at coming up with good solutions to problems like these will affect the quality of life of your kids. The more intelligent you are, the better you will be at coming up with good solutions to problems. Therefore, becoming more intelligent will improve the lives of your kids.

The Desire to be Free

Many outside forces are constantly trying to control us. For example, someone may try to manipulate you into doing something you don't want to do and aren't obligated to do. If you aren't assertive, you will be successfully manipulated. If you are assertive, you are invulnerable to this kind of manipulation. Thus, we see that transforming yourself into an assertive person will free you from manipulation.

The media is also constantly trying to control us via propaganda. Developing astuteness and intelligence will help you recognize any deception woven into such propaganda. Thus, transforming yourself into an astute and intelligent person will free you from the influence of that deception.[11]

Society often forces us to conform to established social roles. For example, at one point in time women were expected to stay at home to take care of the kids without ever pursuing a career of their own. To decide not to conform to these kinds of established social roles takes courage. Thus, transforming yourself into a courageous person frees you from the pressure to conform.

The Desire to be Productive

Laziness and inefficiency, among other negative traits, keep us from being as productive as we otherwise could be. Eliminating those traits from your personality will greatly increase your productivity. Developing traits like organization, efficiency, intelligence, and self-discipline will further increase your productivity. No one wants to die thinking they wasted their life and did nothing significant. However, no one lives forever. We all have a limited amount of time that we can use to do something meaningful. Therefore, it is imperative that we develop the traits we need to make the most out of the precious time we have.

The Desire for Success

Transforming yourself for the better will help you be more successful. Any time we are unsuccessful, some negative trait is usually at the root of our failure. Eliminating those traits is often the first step towards leading a successful life. This should be obvious, so there is no need for me to labor the point.

The Four Types of Control

There are (at least) four types of control that are relevant to the subject of self-transformation, and therefore need to be discussed. Three of them are control of your physical actions, control of your emotions, and control of your personality. The fourth is control of your thoughts, but I will not explicitly discuss this because everything I say about control of emotions also applies to control of thoughts, so I would be repeating myself.

You need to control your physical actions. If your emotions control your physical actions, then you are not in control of your physical actions. If you are angry, then your anger may take control of your physical actions and cause you to punch someone. If you are in control of your physical actions, then you can decide not to punch someone, and there is nothing your anger can do about it because your anger doesn't control your physical actions. This kind of control is very important to have, but can be exhausting to exercise. Sometimes, while you are exercising control over your physical actions, your emotions are trying to wrestle control of your physical actions away from you. This kind of struggle can result in a lot of strain for you.

Often when people say to control your emotions, what they really mean is to control your physical actions so that your emotions don't control your physical actions. When it comes to magical training, because we deal regularly with these subjects, our language and vocabulary need to be precise. Having talked about controlling your physical actions, let's talk about controlling your emotions.

This kind of control is very difficult. If you can control your emotions, it means you can willfully create new emotions, transmute those emotions, and dissolve those emotions. For example, let's say you aren't feeling any emotions. You can cause yourself to feel angry, then transmute that anger into fear, then transmute that fear into joy, and then dissolve that joy into nothingness. If you are feeling angry and want to avoid hurting someone, you can exercise control over your physical actions by forcing yourself not to punch someone out of anger. You can also exercise control over your emotions by transmuting the anger you feel into serenity or dissolving the anger into nothingness. This is the better option. It takes more practice, but developing this skill is part of the Step 2 astral work.

Another kind of control, is control over your personality. This kind of control is exercised by shaping your personality. This can be done by acquiring new personality traits, strengthening existing personality traits, or ridding yourself of personality traits. Anger is an emotion that arises from irritability. If you eliminate the personality trait of irritability, then anger won't be able to rise in you. Thus, exercising control of your personality by eliminating the personality traits that produce anger is the permanent long term solution to the problem of becoming angry and wanting to punch people.

The magician must possess all three kinds of control:

1. Control of one's physical actions

2. Control of one's emotions (and thoughts)

3. Control of one's personality

The student of magic will frequently find himself exercising one or more of these types of control. For example, if you are irritable, you should work on eliminating this trait from your personality. This is exercising control over your personality. However, eliminating a trait takes time. If someone triggers your irritability making you angry and you want to punch that person, you either need to exercise control over your physical actions by restraining yourself from punching the person or control over your emotions by dissolving the anger. Think of anger as a force that is trying to compel you to punch someone. When you exercise control over your physical actions, you apply a different force (the force of your will) to counteract the force of anger. When you exercise control over your emotions, you get rid of the force (of anger) by dissolving it. When you exercise control over your personality, you get rid of the source of the force (irritability) so that the force (anger) cannot be produced in the future.

Microscopic Strategies

Self-transformation strategies fall into three categories, microscopic, mesoscopic, and macroscopic.[12] Macroscopic self-transformation techniques and strategies were the subject of the second chapter of *The Elemental Equilibrium: Notes on the Foundation of Magical Adepthood*. These strategies are designed to root out and eliminate a negative trait over a long period of time, or to build up and develop a positive trait over a long period of time.

For example, let's say you are irritable and get angry easily. Impregnating food with patience and eating it (conscious eating) will root out this trait. However, if you feel really angry and are about to punch someone, you cannot run off to find food, impregnate it with patience, and then eat it. This is not practical. Furthermore, patience is developed by practicing conscious eating over the course of many days and weeks. Impregnating one meal with patience and eating it won't make you instantaneously patient, so even if you could conjure up food whenever you feel angry, impregnate it with patience, and then eat it, this still would not help you control yourself and prevent the anger from taking control of you. For this, you need strategies that function on the microscopic level.

In the second edition of *A Bardon Companion,* Rawn gives the following microscopic strategy:

1. Detach yourself from the emotional desire that compels you to act in a bad way.
2. Begin repeating an autosuggestion affirmation designed to counter the trait.
3. Do a "replacement action." This is an action that replaces the bad action you were going to do.

For example, let's say you are struggling with anger and a coworker makes you so angry you want to punch him.

1. The first thing you do is detach yourself from your anger.
2. The second thing you do is begin repeating the affirmation "I am patient."
3. The third thing you do is go eat a cupcake instead of punching your coworker.

I have found it very helpful to add another step between the first and the second. This step is to remove the emotional desire from yourself. Thus, in the example, you would first detach yourself from your anger, then remove the anger from yourself, then begin repeating "I am patient," and then go eat a cupcake. In addition to the magical exhalation, you can also go to a nearby sink and use the magic of water to wash away the negative emotion and trait before proceeding with auto-suggestion and the replacement action. The modified strategy is summarized below:

1. Detach yourself from the emotional desire that compels you to act in a bad way.
2. Remove the emotional desire from yourself.
3. Begin repeating an autosuggestion affirmation designed to counter the trait.

4. Do a "replacement action." This is an action that replaces the bad action you were going to do

To detach yourself from an emotional desire involves realizing it is not a part of you. If you put a rock in your mouth, the rock is inside of you, but it is not a part of you. The emotional desire is the same way. Once you detach yourself from the emotional desire, you greatly limit its ability to control your actions. You go from thinking "I am angry" to thinking "There is anger inside of me." The negative emotion is something foreign to who you really are, and you don't want anything to do with it. Thus, you're not going to let it dictate what you do. Once the negative emotion is viewed in this way, it normally begins to dissipate slowly on its own.

However, instead of letting it dissipate on its own, you can expel it. This is the second step in the modified strategy.

So, how do we remove the emotional desire from ourselves once we detach ourselves from it? There are a number of ways this can be done, but I am going to discuss only three of them.

The first way is to breathe out the emotional desire. You can do this by exhaling several times, letting a portion of the emotional desire flow out from you with each exhalation until it is completely removed. You can also use what I call the IHME and exhale the entirety of the emotional desire at once. This was discussed in *The Elemental Equilibrium: Notes on the Foundation of Magical Adepthood*.

The second way is to go to a sink and use magical washing to wash the emotional desire out of you and down the drain. The obvious disadvantage with this way is that there isn't always going to be a sink nearby. However, if there is a sink nearby and you are proficient in using magical washing, this is certainly a viable option.

The third way is inspired by a trans-personal psychology technique called focusing.[13] The idea here is that the emotional desire produces a physical sensation in your body. There's a good chance this physical sensation will be centered either in your chest or gut. The first thing you do is become aware of the physical sensation in your body caused by the emotional desire. The physical sensation and emotional desire are woven together. For this reason, in focusing, this physical sensation is used to gain deeper insight into the emotional desire. For our purposes, however, we're not going to do that.

Once you have identified the physical sensation and become aware of it, stretch a bit. This loosens up your body and makes it easier for the physical sensation and emotional desire flow. Then, let the physical sensation and the emotional desire giving rise to it flow through your body and into your hands. Then, shake your hands as if you were flicking water from them. As you do this, flick the physical sensation and the emotional desire giving rise to it away from your body.

Once you've become aware of the physical sensation in your body arising from the emotional desire, you can also cause it to flow into your head before breathing it out. This might make breathing it out easier, but is not necessary. You can breathe out the emotional desire directly without first causing it to flow to your head near your nose.

Additional Microscopic Method 1: Role Models

Ok, let's say that your irritability has been triggered and has produced the emotional desire known as anger. This anger compels you to hit or shout at someone. You try to expel the anger from yourself by breathing it out but are only partly successful. You are less angry, but you are still angry, and the anger within you is still trying to take control of your actions and cause you to hit and shout at someone. What do you do?

In the modified strategy discussed in the previous section, you would begin repeating an autosuggestion affirmation and then do a replacement action. For example, you could begin repeating the affirmation "I am patient" and then begin playing video games. You can't simultaneously hit people while playing video games, so playing video games keeps you from hitting people until your anger has dissipated. This is the idea behind the replacement action.

However, there are possible instances where these options are not viable or are not enough. For example, let's say you are in the middle of a meeting. You can't begin repeating "I am patient" to yourself because others will hear. You also can't go play video games because you have to remain at the meeting. Are there other methods for keeping your anger from taking control of you? Yes, there are.

One method is to think about an inspiring role model who is a paragon of the positive trait that is the opposite of the passion giving rise to the emotional desire. For example, the passion giving rise to your anger is irritability. The opposite of irritability is patience. Chojun Miyagi was a very patient man. He once said "When your temper rises, lower your fists—when your fists rise, lower your temper." He also said, "Do not strike others, and do not allow others to strike you. The goal is peace without incident." Regarding this latter quote, we must remember that the idea of striking others includes verbal strikes as well as physical strikes. Anyhow, if you find Chojun Miyagi to be an inspiring person, thinking about his patience and these quotes by him may inspire you to refrain from lashing out in anger. The inspiring role model does not have to be a real person. They can also be from books or movies. For example, the character Yoda in Star Wars is also very patient.

If the role model is really inspiring, then thinking about the role model may be enough. However, it can also help to take this technique to another more magical level by not just thinking about the role model, but imagining you are the role model. Thinking about Yoda may inspire you to be patient, but imagining you're Yoda will give you the patience of Yoda because to some extent, whatever you imagine is real.

Additional Microscopic Method 2: Contemplation of Benefits and Consequences

Another method is to think about all the benefits of preventing the emotional desire from taking control of you, and to think about all the negative consequences of failing to prevent the emotional desire from taking control of you. For example, let's say that someone says something to make you angry at an important meeting. The benefits of controlling yourself include gaining respect from others by remaining patient and composed, and strengthening your willpower by forcing yourself to act calmly. The negative consequences of failing to prevent the anger from causing you to lash out include losing the respect of those around you and maybe even losing your job.

Let's say that it's not anger that is moving you to act unwisely, but fear. Of course, sometimes fear keeps us from doing stupid things like putting ourselves in reckless danger, but other times fear prevents us from truly living. For example, if there is a woman you are in love with, fear of rejection may prevent you from asking her out. However, if you allow fear to prevent you from asking her out, you have no chance of developing a relationship with her. You can think about the benefits of preventing fear from taking control of you, and thinking about the negative consequences of letting fear remain in control of you. One benefit is that you get some practice at asking women out, so that even if she rejects you, you will be more comfortable doing something like this again in the future. Another benefit is that you learn that you are in fact capable of overcoming your fears, and knowing this fact will help you overcome your fears in the future, even in situations that don't involve dating. For example, if you are afraid of asking your boss for a promotion, you are more likely to be able to overcome this fear because you have overcome your fear before. As for the negative consequences of letting your fear control you, there are several. Most of them center on the fact that if you let your fear control you, you will be prevented from living an exciting life. Again, I'm not talking about fear of loss of life or limb. That kind of fear prevents you from doing stupid stuff that leads to a preventable death. I'm talking about fear of rejection, fear of social interactions, fear of change, fear of the unknown, etc. These are the kinds of fears that may lock us into boring predictable lives.

Note that this is indeed a method that functions on the temporal microscopic level. If you are at a bar and you see a woman you want to ask out but are afraid to do so, you can't buy food, impregnate it with courage, eat it, become courageous as a result, and then ask her out. You need a method that will instantly make your more courageous. Contemplating the benefits of being courageous and the negative consequences of remaining fearful may move you to act courageously and ask her out.

Additional Microscopic Method 3: Imagine You're Dead

Another method is to imagine that you are dead and reflecting back on the incarnation you have just finished living. Let's say that someone steals a pencil from you and you are so angry that you want to lash out at them verbally. If you do this, will you not be ashamed when you think about this incident during your review of your life? This method helps put things into perspective. It helps you see that life is valuable, and it also helps you see the relative value of everything in your life. Sometimes a trivial thing might seem worth getting upset over, but when you look at it from a larger perspective, you realize it is not worth getting upset over at all. This exercise gives you that larger perspective. When you die and then reflect back on the life you've just lived, you don't want to be ashamed of that life. This method reminds you of that fact by actually putting you in the position of reflecting back on your life. In this way, it moves you to act in a manner that is not shameful.

Additional Microscopic Method 4: Imagine You're Your Guardian Angel

Another method is to imagine that you're your Holy Guardian Angel. This is the being whose job it is to guide you in acting wisely and righteously. The previous method gave you a new view on the situation—a bigger view. This method also gives you a new view on the situation—a divine view. Oftentimes, a new view is all that is needed in order to change our behavior. For example, if we are acting rude but don't think we are being rude, it might help if someone videotapes us and then shows us the video. Looking at the video allows you to see yourself from the perspective of others. After watching the video of yourself, you might think to yourself "Wow, I really am rude." Whether you are viewing yourself from the perspective of your future dead self as in the last method, your HGA (Higher Guardian Angel) as in this method, or someone/something else, know that the very act of viewing yourself from a new perspective provides new insights that may help you change your behavior.

For example, let's say that I have found a wallet lying around. There is no one around, and there are no cameras around. I could easily steal the cash in the wallet and get away with it. My greed compels me to do this. Of course, I can't just go impregnate food with selflessness and eat it in order to overcome the greed. Yeah, if I ate food impregnated with selflessness every day for a few weeks I'd become selfless and my greed would be gone, but that fact doesn't help me right now. The wallet is right in front of me, and I'm trying to keep myself from stealing the cash in it. I could use the first method and imagine I am a selfless person like the monk who gave the thief his robe.[14] I could use the second method and contemplate the benefits of not touching the wallet and the negative consequences of stealing the cash inside. I could use the fourth method and imagine I'm my own guardian angel. As my guardian angel, I look at myself and facepalm. I think to myself "Wow, this person has a long way to go as far as his spiritual development goes. He can't even control his urge to steal, yet he fantasizes about controlling the elements. Hahaha." Seeing myself from the perspective of my HGA suddenly causes me to not want to steal the cash inside the wallet.

Additional Microscopic Method 5: Enter the Void

If a negative emotion is compelling you to act in an unwise manner (e.g. if anger is compelling you to hit someone or greed is compelling you to steal), enter the void and let the void dissolve the negative emotion. Entering the void often also leads to clarity of mind, which lets you think rationally. This in turns makes you more likely to act rationally instead of impulsively.

Chapter 9: Kindness

In each section of TRFSS(EV), Bill presents a challenge, as well as some magical practices designed to prepare you to meet that challenge. The challenge presented in the Jupiter/Chesed section is as follows:

> *"Life is short, yet every individual is given opportunities to be of benefit to others. Leave the world a better place than the one you entered."*

The practice Bill gives to help you meet this challenge is literally just to work through IIH. Bill clearly views IIH as a training manual that prepares you to "leave the world a better place than the one you entered."

Remember the Malkuth exercise from the previous chapter where you make your life into a story worth telling? Remember how I explained that IIH helps you develop the stylus, sharpening knife, ink holder, and paperweight needed to write the story of your life? The idea here is that you arrange the plot of the story in such a way that the protagonist (you) improves the world.

Think about Moana. She helped her society a lot by saving it from the darkness caused by the absence of the heart of Te Fiti. Furthermore, she helped her society rediscover its love for voyaging and taught them the knowledge of wayfaring. In *How To Train Your Dragon*, Hiccup greatly helps his society by ending years of war between his people and the dragons.

Hiccup's story and Moana's story are both interesting and entertaining. Clearly, if you're going to write out a destiny for yourself that also happens to be a story worth telling, it's a wise idea to plot out the story in such a way that you leave the world better off than it was before. In the fields of literature and anthropology, many stories are believed to follow a general template identified by Joseph Campbell and known as the "hero's journey." In *The Hero with a Thousand Faces*, Campbell states that at the end of such stories, the main character gains and uses "the power to bestow boons on his fellow man." In other words, he helps his society and leaves the world, or at least his corner of the world, a better place than the one he entered.

Many people begin their study of esoteric disciplines because they want to use practical magic to improve the world. I was one of those people. I had always fantasized about having my own room in my house that was a permanent magical oratory. There would be a circle painted on the ground with an altar in the center. Sigils and mystical designs would be etched on the walls. I would perform long complex rituals to manifest world peace, eliminate poverty, and increase the use of clean energy. That was how I envisioned myself working as a magician. It's actually not an unrealistic image; however, you need to realize that the primary forces powering such magic are the electric and magnetic fluids. All magical energies, whether they are elemental, planetary, zodiacal, or whatever, either derive from or relate to these primary forces. Therefore, in order to use practical magic effectively, you need to first master the wisdom and lessons pertaining to each of these two fluids.

When it comes to practical magic, the electric fluid tries to teach you it's wisdom by asking you a question. That question, as Bill puts it, is as follows:

> *"The question the electrical fluid will ask you in terms of your faith and conviction is 'Are you willing to work without using magic to attain what you want if we set a clear path before you?' You want money? Are you willing to work for it? Here is a job. Do you want love? Are you willing to first give the love you want to others? You want to succeed in life? Are you willing to prepare yourself so that you will be ready to seize the opportunity when it comes to you? The electrical likes to check up on just how much you really want what you are asking for."*

All magicians want human society to be filled with joy, wonder, and prosperity. However, the magicians who will actually contribute to making this happen will be those who use mundane methods as readily as they use magical methods. So, how do you use mundane methods to improve the world? You could start by learning to treat others with kindness at every opportunity you get to do so. Compliment others. Give people the support they need to succeed. Learn to listen empathically when people need to get something off their chests. Go out of your way to make someone's day. Do what you can to prevent people from experiencing unnecessary suffering. Strive to be a source of joy to others.

To improve society is to change society. To change anything, it is necessary to have power. There are many forms of power. If you are rich, you have a lot of money. You can use that money to build high quality schools and orphanages, start organizations designed to benefit the world, and create scholarships. Money is a form of power, and any form of power can be used to change the world for the better. If you are a famous person, you can tell your fans to take care of the environment. People will do what you tell them to do just because you are famous. Fame is another form of power. If you are very knowledgeable, you can invent machines that purify water at a cheaper cost, design new and more effective agricultural strategies, and come up with transportation models that make travel more efficient, therefore saving everyone time and reducing air pollution. Knowledge is another form of power.

Magic is the art of using power wisely. In other words, it's the art of using power to carry out the will of Divine Providence. In other words, it's about using power to make the world a better place; after all, that's what Divine Providence wants.

Some people don't have a lot of power. They don't have a lot of money or fame, or are not well-educated. They may feel that they can't improve the world very much because of how little power they have. The thing is, everyone possesses the quality of kindness to some degree, and kindness is also a form of power. This was the great secret Cinderella's mother revealed to her before she died.

"Have courage and be kind. You have more kindness in your little finger than most people possess in their whole body. And it has power. More than you know."

When you do what you can with what power you have, God will reward you with more power. This is one key to acquiring more power, and it does apply to magical power.

The more progress you make in your magical training, the more magical power you will have. When you practice your magical exercises, you are trying to increase your magical power. Thus, practicing your magical exercises can be seen as a way of asking Divine Providence for more magical power. Many people practice their magical exercises but get no better. Divine Providence denies their request for more magical power, so they remain stuck on Step 1 for years, never advancing to Step 2. Their lack of progress causes them to become frustrated and to give up.

To gain more magical power, you must show Divine Providence that you are worthy of more magical power. You already have magical power in the form of kindness. Previously I stated that kindness is mundane, which is true. There are many kind people who don't have the slightest interest in any esoteric discipline, and regular acts of kindness should be a part of everyone's mundane day-to-day life. However, despite this, kindness is profoundly magical. The magician is one who strives to become a co-creator of the universe. This requires him to embody the attributes of Divinity. In Step 10 of IIH, we find instructions for doing just that with the help of an elemental model of Divinity, where omnipotence is reflected in the fiery quality of Divinity, omniscience is reflected in the airy quality of Divinity, etc. However, a sephirothic model of Divinity can also be used for many magical purposes. In this case, the quality reflected in the Chesed aspect of Divinity is loving-kindness. In his list of beatitudes, Bill writes that "Blessed are those who find the divine within themselves, for they shall create peace and justice shall fill the earth." When it comes to finding the divine within yourself, the first step is not to practice weird breathing exercises or to chant mantras, or to practice fancy rituals. The first step is to begin expressing the divine qualities that are already in your personality in order to strengthen them. Kindness is one of those qualities. It's divine, and therefore magical.

If you don't actively use the magical power that is kindness, Divine Providence will think "You haven't shown me you can use the magical power you already have; why should I give you more?" As soon as you start using the magical power of kindness, Divine Providence thinks "Ah, it is clear that if I invest magical power in this person, I will get a good return on my investment." As a result, Divine Providence will give you more magical power. This manifests as progress in your training, after all, the further along in your magical training you are, the more magical power you have. You will smoothly glide through the process of learning to accumulate, condense, and project magical energies.

Now, at this point, you might be asking how you can be sure I am telling the truth when I claim that you must be a kind person in order to advance past Step 1. For all you know, I could have just pulled that claim out of my ass. For now, let's ignore the fact that Bardon repeatedly hints at the importance of kindness throughout the text of IIH and consider two passages about fairy tales from his books. The following passage comes from IIH,

> *"But neither fairy tales nor sagas exist for the true adept, because they are to be understood as a sort of symbolism concealing many deep truths."*

The following passage comes from KTQ.

> *"For someone initiated into magic and Quabbalah who understands the symbolic language, fairy tales reveal many mysteries, since he is used to looking at all events with quite different eyes than common people do. A hermetic will not be surprised to realize that he was already fond of fairy tales in his childhood, and that he still likes to reflect on their content in later years, since*

he understands their high and true sense which can only be read between the lines."

So we see from these two passages that fairy tales often contain profound magical truths. There are numerous of fairy tales that portray kindness as either a magical power or a necessary prerequisite for magical advancement. In fact, my favorite fairy tale "The Fool of the World and the Flying Ship" is one of them.[15] In this story, there is a king will tells everyone in his kingdom that whoever brings him a flying ship will be allowed to marry his daughter. In the kingdom there is a family consisting of a father, a mother, and three sons. The two oldest sons are extremely intelligent. They set off on a journey to obtain a flying ship and are never heard from again. The youngest son isn't too bright, but he is very kind. He also sets off on a journey to obtain a flying ship. Along the way, he meets and old man and treats the old man with kindness. The old man then tells the youngest son how to obtain a flying ship.

One detail to contemplate is that in this story, the youngest son treats the old man with kindness by sharing his food with him. When the youngest son started his journey, all the he had to eat were "some crusts of dry black bread and a flask of water." However, when he opens his bag to share this food with the old man, he sees "fresh white rolls and cooked meats." Furthermore, when he pours out the contents of the flask so the old man can have some, "instead of water there came out corn brandy, and that of the best." The youngest son demonstrated his ability to have the power to make others happy (magical power), which is represented by the quality of the food he can share with others, instantly increases once he begins using this power. The old man remarks that this better food/more magical power is "what God has given."

The word "initiation" is a popular buzzword that is thrown around all the time in modern esotericism. It means different things to different people. In the Bardon system, it has a very specific meaning. Initiation is the process of learning to exteriorize one's subtle bodies. An initiate is someone who is proficient in exteriorizing his subtle bodies. Daskalos and Blavatsky use the same definition of initiation. Hermes, the archetypal initiate, possesses winged sandals that symbolize his ability to fly through the inner planes via mental wandering.

When it comes to ways you can improve the world, your options will greatly increase once you complete your initiation; that is to say, once you have worked through the first eight steps of IIH. Each of the ruling genii of the Earthzone can provide you with the knowledge and guidance needed to further the evolution of some aspect of human science, technology, art, or culture. Regardless of which spirits you work with or how you work with them, note that the magic you do will be genuine and ring with divine potency. In one of his essays, Bill talks about his work with the Earthzone spirit Cigila and mentions that Cigila gave him "specific information on location, incidents, and the disasters that were to be and that could still be adverted." As a result of this information, he was able to "intervene in ways which [...] stopped a nuclear exchange and a few cities from being nuked."

Learning from the Earthzone spirits and working alongside them to recreate the world into a better place is an enjoyable and enriching experience. To engage in this work, you first need to learn to exteriorize your mental body—a skill developed in Step 8. However, if you do not develop kindness and exercise it, you will never advance past Step 1. Realize that if the Fool had never shared his food with the ancient old man, he would never have obtained the flying ship.

Go get that flying ship!

Chapter 10: Saturn

Working with Personal Karma

One of the unique aspects of the literature surrounding the Bardon system that has been created by its students is the prevalence of writings about karma. In some magical traditions, the extent to which karma is discussed is more or less "If you do bad things, bad things will happen to you." That's true enough, but the subject of karma can be a lot deeper, more interesting, and more multi-faceted than that.

In the past, I thought that once you had created negative karma for yourself, there was nothing you could do about it. You'd just have to wait until that karma hit you and then suffer through it. When I began to study the literature of the Bardon system, I encountered many things that blew my mind. For example, in *Memories of Franz Bardon*, there is that famous story about Bardon taking the negative karma of a girl upon himself in order to cure her of tuberculosis, but then giving the negative karma back when he found that it was too much of a burden and would interfere too much with his life's work. From this story, I learned that karma can be moved from person to person.

I also learned that karma can also be actively worked with. While karma is always karma, the way karma manifests in your life is variable. Oftentimes, through various mundane and magical methods, it's possible to influence the way the karma manifests. This isn't the same as getting rid of your karma or escaping from it. You're working through your karma just like everyone else is working through your karma. The big difference is that you have some say in regards to how you will work through your karma. If you don't like to suffer, you can arrange to work through some of your karma in a way that has less suffering.

The idea that we have some say over how we work through our karma is central to many divine missions. The Earthzone spirit in charge of divine missions is Cigila. Bill begins his essay on this spirit by writing the following.[16]

> "Cigila is one of the first spirits I worked with decades ago. I immediately had a prophetic dream about a world event which Cigila wished to prevent. Karma can be like a balloon payment in which all the debt comes due at once. In this case, it causes terrible suffering. On the other hand, karma can also be satisfied in ways which are relatively mild and which bring fulfillment to all concerned. Cigila specializes in unfolding the future so it becomes a path of light, love, and wisdom."

The idea here is that karma is a teacher. When you do something bad, you create negative karma for yourself. This negative karma serves as negative reinforcement that teaches you not to do the bad thing again. When you do something good, you create positive karma for yourself. This positive karma serves as positive reinforcement that teaches you to continue doing the good thing whenever you have the opportunity to so. In the end, the reason for karma's existence is to get you to learn.

Negative karma usually causes suffering. Sometimes it manifest slowly as a long period of mild suffering. Other times, it manifests suddenly as an intense event that causes massive suffering at once. This is what Bill means when he writes that karma can be like a balloon payment. A large part of the negative group karma of the human race, for whatever reason, was scheduled to come due at once in the form of a nuclear explosion. Cigila warned Bill about this in a dream and instructed him to use magical techniques to work with the karma so that it would come due in a different, more gradual, and less violent manner. This kind of work is a form of genuine service. By engaging with negative karma and consciously working with it, a skilled magician can get it to manifest in a way saturated with "light, love, and wisdom."

In IIH, Bardon writes that Cigila prefers to work with magicians who have had extensive magical training in past lives. After working with Cigila, Bill discovered the reason for this preference and explains it as follows.

"The reason Cigila prefers individuals who have been magicians in previous lifetimes is because his level of power requires someone who has already worked through the basic issues of magic. [...] The ability to take hold of karma and transform it through spiritual will, this too is a basic requirement."

The thing is, when it comes to the basic issues of magic such as the ability to take hold of karma and transform it, the Bardon system of training already has all of that covered. If you read through IIH, you won't find any exercises for working with karma, but if you begin the process of working through IIH, you will quickly encounter issues that center on karma and you will be required to work through those issues in order to advance. This shouldn't be surprising. The microcosm and the macrocosm reflect each other. Therefore, learning to work with your own personal karma also teaches you how to work with the group karma of the human race.

Whenever you do anything bad, you create negative karma for yourself. The only way to get rid of this karma is to work through it. Depending on how that karma manifests in your life, working through the negative karma can be more or less unpleasant. To mitigate the suffering you will experience when you work through the karma, take the following steps. They will lessen the amount of karma you create for yourself and make it more likely that you will work through the karma in a more pleasant manner than you would have if you hadn't taken these steps. Whenever you commit a wrongdoing that creates negative karma for you…

1. Acknowledge that you have done what you did.
2. Acknowledge that what you did was wrong.
3. Do something to counteract the negative effect of your wrongdoing.
4. Take measures to ensure that you do not do that wrongdoing or any similar wrongdoing in the future.

For example, let's say you have willed someone to suffer misfortune. Perhaps he was annoying you and your ill will was fueled by anger. Perhaps he has something you don't have and your ill will was fueled by envy.

The first thing you must do is acknowledge that you have willed him to suffer misfortune. The second thing you must do is acknowledge that willing him to suffer misfortune was wrong. These two steps are pretty straightforward.

The third thing you must do is take measures to counteract the negative effect of what you did. Remember that the power of your will can create currents and forms on the inner planes. Thus, willing someone to suffer misfortune will cause them to suffer misfortune. Use the power of your imagination to travel back in time to the moment right before you willed him to suffer misfortune. Then, at the moment in time when you willed him to suffer misfortune, emanate compassionate love toward him instead. After returning to the present-moment via your imagination, say a prayer to the Most High asking that his life be blessed.

Finally, take measures to ensure that you don't do anything similar in the future. First, identify what negative trait caused you to will him to suffer misfortune (irritability, envy, sadism, etc.). Then, if that that negative trait is not in your black soul mirror, write it in your black soul mirror. Finally, use the six-pronged attack to root out the negative trait. If you are already applying the full force of the Six-Pronged Attack toward rooting out another negative trait, you don't have to work on rooting out this negative trait immediately; however, you should make concrete plans to.

Instead of a mental wrongdoing, let's examine a physical wrongdoing. Let's say you enjoy knocking the cups out of the hands of homeless people because you think it is entertaining to watch them scramble around on the ground collecting all the money that has spilled out.

After doing this, you should first acknowledge that you have done it and acknowledge that it was wrong. Then, you should pay the homeless person the amount of money equal to the money that was blown away by the wind before he could pick it up. In addition, you should give him some more money than that to compensate for the stress and energy involved in scrambling around to pick up the money that spilled from the cup after you knocked it out of his hands. Finally, you should use the Six-Pronged Attack to develop compassion, or at the very least, make plans to do so in the near future.

Let's examine one more example. In this example, you get angry at someone and burn his house down. The first thing you should do is acknowledge that you have burned his house down. The second thing to do is to acknowledge that burning his house down was wrong. The third thing you should do is buy him a new house. The fourth thing you should do is take measures to ensure that you don't commit any acts of arson again in the future. This involves using the Six-Pronged Attack to root out the personality traits (like irritability) that cause you to set peoples' houses on fire.

Always stay present-minded. If you are absent-minded, you won't remember to take these four steps whenever you do something wrong. However, if you are present-minded, you will realize you have committed a wrongdoing whenever you commit a wrongdoing and be able to take these four measures to prevent mistakes in future.

Responsibility

Responsibility is the virtue that corresponds most with Saturn. If you examine a variety of planetary tables of correspondences and look at the virtues assigned to Saturn, responsibility is always on there, and it is almost always the first trait listed. Needless to say, one of the lessons Saturn has to teach us about maturity is that in order to be mature, you must be responsible.

It's very easy to say to yourself, "I'm going to take responsibility for the world by doing my part to end wars and establish peace and justice." That's great. But for the most part, those are empty words. When it comes to taking on responsibilities, you need to start small and then work your way up to big things. That isn't to say that you shouldn't try to make the world a better place. On the contrary, you should continually strive to make the world a better place. However, deciding to take responsibility for the state of the world and of human society doesn't really impress Saturn unless you have a coherent conscious and subconscious understanding of everything involved in doing that. Divine missions are big responsibilities, but when it comes to becoming a responsible person at the beginning of your training, you don't start by taking on divine missions. You start smaller and closer to home.

When it comes to beginning the process of becoming responsible, we need to look at two processes.

1. Taking responsibility for yourself
2. Fulfilling the responsibilities of your day to day life

Those of you who are familiar with Bill's approach for finding Saturn within yourself know that the first step in that approach is "to take responsibility for who you are." In other words, take responsibility for all aspects of yourself.[17] To do this, it's necessary to first know yourself. In Bill's description of the first step, he makes several comments on what it means to know yourself. For example, he writes that "to know yourself is to know something of the forces which move the universe" and that "to know yourself is to attain union with the world." Obviously, knowing yourself begins with creating the soul mirrors and then studying your soul mirrors after creating them.

Acquiring knowledge of yourself isn't the same as taking responsibility for yourself. It just puts you in a better position to take responsibility for yourself because it teaches you what you need to know about yourself in order to take responsibility for yourself. Actually taking responsibility for yourself begins with establishing an elemental equilibrium. While explaining the first step of taking responsibility for yourself, Bill writes that Saturn's inner source of inspiration is "a knowledge of equilibrium and inner harmony so the universe can be reflected in yourself without distortion or impurity." This knowledge of equilibrium doesn't come from reading about equilibrium. It comes from experiencing equilibrium. The whole universe is in equilibrium, so when you do establish equilibrium within yourself, you'll find that you reflect the nature of the universe.

Acquiring knowledge of yourself and then establishing an elemental equilibrium is the work of the first two steps of IIH. So, we see that right at the beginning of IIH, Bardon asks the student to take responsibility for himself in anticipation of the far greater responsibilities he will take once he finishes his training and begins working as a magician to "build a world in which the highest ideals of spirit and Divine Providence are fully present and realized."

Regarding the second process of fulfilling the responsibilities of your day to day life, this is extremely important. One way to become a responsible person is to act like a responsible person, and responsible people fulfill their responsibilities. As an exercise, think about the various roles you currently hold (employee, father, friend, etc.). Think about the responsibilities that come with each role and reflect on how well you fulfill those responsibilities. Then, take note of the ways in which you can fulfill those responsibilities even better, or if you are not fulfilling them at all, how you can begin to fulfill them.

Learning to fulfill my various responsibilities was a big struggle for me because I used to be a very lazy person. When I was in grade school, I never wanted to be the leader when we were assigned group projects. The leader always has extra responsibilities, and responsibilities can be heavy burdens. Therefore, a lazy person like me actively avoided unnecessary responsibilities. Some people were ambitious and always wanted to be the leader. Their ambition gave them the energy to carry those extra responsibilities. However, my own lazy self didn't want to do that. When I was working through Step 2, I had to root out my laziness, become responsible, and develop better leadership skills. That was difficult, but it taught me a lot.

For example, it taught me a lot about the importance of taking on new roles. The role of the leader comes with certain responsibilities, and therefore when you take on the role of a leader, you learn many things about responsibility and about how to be responsible. When I was contemplating this one day, I realized that every role has its responsibilities. Therefore, every role has something unique to teach you about responsibility, how to be responsible, and where you stand in terms of being a responsible person. I took on some leadership roles to improve my leadership skills, but when I had finished with that, I sought to take on other roles too. I found the lessons about responsibility that the various roles taught me fascinating.

The more I explored the concept of responsibility, the more I came to understand one of the paradoxes surrounding this concept. Saturn exists to help us become free. To fully master the lessons pertaining to Saturn is to become free and liberated. However, a large portion of the process of learning Saturn's lessons consists of fulfilling your responsibilities. That might seem strange; after all, responsibilities are kind of like burdens. They restrict you and prevent you from doing many things you want to do. For example, a couple who doesn't have any children may be able to go out whenever they want. However, once they have kids, their parental responsibilities prevent them from doing that. They have to worry about stuff like finding a baby sitter, taking care of their children when they are sick, etc.

However, in the end, fulfilling responsibilities does free you because fulfilling responsibilities teaches you to be responsible, and to be responsible is to be responsible for yourself and for the world in which you live. When you take responsibility for yourself, you can shape yourself into however you want to be. This means you free yourself from all of the external entities, organizations, and powers that are trying to shape you to be a certain way in order to fulfill their own agendas. When you take responsibility for the world, you can free it from the darkness that tries to corrupt it. This is why Saturn, the planet that teaches you about responsibility, is also the planet that teaches you how to limit malice and negativity.

Chapter 11: Taking on New Roles

"Great actors make a point of taking parts they have never played before because they want to grow. They are committed to their art."
~William Mistele

The university I attended had several engineering programs; electrical engineering, mechanical engineering, civil engineering, chemical engineering, etc. Several of these engineering programs required students to take this one really hard introductory programming course. I was in an engineering program that did not require students to take that programming course. I had heard that the course was extremely difficult and extremely time consuming. Still, despite not being required to take this class, and despite having no prior experience or interest in programming, I was compelled by some unknown force to register for the course anyway during the second semester of my freshman year.

That semester sucked. Taking that course was one the hardest thing I have ever done. It was so time-consuming that I had little time for any sort of leisure or relaxation. I programmed for long hours into the night pretty much every night. There were many times I felt like smashing the computer against the wall out of frustration.

However, although I hated every aspect of that course, and although that semester was filled with nothing but suffering, I'm glad I took that course because I know that if I hadn't taken it, I would never have successfully worked through IIH. Why? You're probably sick of me saying this, but a magician is not just someone with magical skills and abilities. My experience taking that course provided me with a lot of the other stuff required of a student in order to become a magician. That stuff isn't the kind of stuff you get by reading books about magic or sitting in your asana practicing magical exercises.

Since the course was extremely time consuming, I had to become an expert in managing and budgeting my time. Learning about recursion and functional programming taught me to think in new and unusual ways. I got a very low grade on the first exam and was convinced that I would fail the course. I ended up passing the course with a relatively high grade. This taught me that I am capable of accomplishing much more than I previously thought I could. I wasn't intelligent enough to program, but through hard work and effort, I became intelligent enough to program. That programming course challenged me in such a way that I was forced to develop inner strength and overcome my limitations in order to make it. It's what hermetic magicians these days call a "crucible." It's not the only crucible I've been through, but it's the one I've chosen to write about here because it's the least personal. Without the inner strength, self-discipline, confidence in my ability to overcome my limitations, knowledge of time management, and new ways of thinking that the programming course provided me with, I would not be nearly as successful in life, and I would never have succeeded in my magical training.

Now, I said that the programming course was time-consuming. Since I wasn't required to take the course, I could have very easily taken a much easier course that required little work and consumed almost no time. I did know of a few courses that were like that. For example, there was one course in which the professors regularly canceled class, assigned no homework, and gave one very easy final exam at the end of the semester. I could have taken that instead. The work I had to do for the programming course I took consumed a few hours of my time each day. If I had taken an easier course instead, I could have had several more hours of free time each day. Imagine if I had done that and used those hours of free time to read books about magic. I could have read numerous books by people like Dion Fortune, Aleister Crowley, Israel Regardie, Paul Foster Case, Eliphas Levi, Annie Besant, Alice Bailey, Samuel Mathers, and Arthur Edward Waite. I could have read book after book about divination, ritual magic, hoodoo, talismans, witchcraft, alchemy, astrology, Qabbalah, and Tarot symbolism. If I had done that, I would probably still be on Step 1 right now.

Time management is a central part of magical training. There is no one who is more aware of the limited time he has in his short lifespan to grow, evolve, and make the world a better place than the magician. In The Last Lecture, Randy Pausch states that "Time must be explicitly managed, like money." All students of Bardon's system who have completed IIH succeeded in completing IIH because they realized this truth very early on in their training. When it comes to the subject of reading, it is clear that the right amount of time must be spent reading, but the key idea here is "the right amount of time." If you spend too little time reading, you could be missing out on some very helpful information. If you spend too much time reading, then you are wasting your time.

There are several concentration exercises in IIH. The Bardonist would do very well to read a book or two about concentration. Mouni Sadhu's Concentration: *A Guide to Mental Mastery* is excellent. Swami Sivananda has also written some great books on the subject. However, does the Bardonist need to read ten books about concentration? No, he doesn't. Similarly, visualization training is part of the work of IIH. The Bardonist would do well to read some articles about visualization. However, does he need to read one hundred articles about visualization? No, he doesn't. There are much better uses for one's time than that. Consider, for example, using your time by taking on new roles.

Part of the reason you incarnate is to learn and evolve. As Shakespeare once wrote, "All the world's a stage, and all the men and women merely players." Life is a stage. You're an actor. As Bill wrote in his essay on the electric fluid, "Great actors make a point of taking parts they have never played before because they want to grow. They are committed to their art." I took on a role as programming student. It was a role I'd never played before, and therefore, that role did a lot to help me grow. When it comes to spiritual evolution, taking on new roles forms the basics. Chanting mantras, vibrating divine names, visualizing Hebrew letters, and meditating come later, if at all. Such exercises are unproductive if practiced before one's soul and spirit are ready to reap whatever benefits they can provide. When you take on new roles, you draw upon parts of your soul and spirit that you previously had never drawn upon before. This develops those parts of your soul and spirit. When you continually play the same role, you develop the same parts of your soul and spirit. This isn't inherently bad, but if you don't develop the other parts of your soul and spirit, your soul and spirit become unbalanced. In magic, a lack of balance is a source of weakness and a gateway to danger. Power and strength arise from balance. Take on a variety of different roles in life so you can develop all parts of your soul and spirit.

As of now, my life is very busy and thus I find myself with no free time. If I ever did find myself with free time, instead of buying occult or esoteric books and reading them, I'd learn figure skating. I've never had the chance to take on a role that was anything similar to that of a figure skater, and so I have reason to believe that taking on the role of a figure skater would do a lot for my personal development. I have studied a few others arts in my life though, including acting, piano, guitar, creative writing, and Shotokan. In other words, I've taken on the role of the actor, the piano player, the guitar player, the writer, and the martial artist. In the process of taking on those roles, I've not only developed different parts of my being, I've also learned a lot about who I am.

That's the other thing about taking on different roles. The phrase "Know thyself" was written over the front door of the Temple of Apollo. Since then, teachers of magic and of related esoteric disciplines have urged their students to do just that—to know themselves. It is our experiences in life that teach us about ourselves. The experience of writing my first book taught me a lot about myself. In other words, taking on the role of an author taught me a lot about myself. For one thing, I learned that I am capable of writing a book. I learned that I do not brainstorm and plan out chapters before jumping in to write them. I learned that I have trouble deciding to declare a book finished and to move on to new writing projects.

When you take on new roles, you undergo new experiences. When you undergo new experiences, you learn new things about yourself. This helps you know yourself. Don't believe me? The next time you undergo a new experience, reflect back on the experience and ask yourself whether or not you can think of some new items to put on your soul mirrors. You might flirt with someone for the first time and, after reflecting on this experience, realize you are bad at flirting and put this on your black soul mirror. Or, you might take a salsa dancing class and realize you have some kind of innate talent for it. Were this to happen, you could then put this on your white soul mirror.

Some people were born with amazing psychic abilities, or had cool magical experiences while growing up. One woman I know talked to fairies regularly throughout her childhood. A good friend of mine was born with a highly developed inner sense of smell. I've also met people who were born telepathic, or who were visited by angels while growing up, or who regularly have precognitive dreams. I wasn't born with any psychic abilities. I didn't have any cool magical experiences until I was pretty far into my magical training. At one point, I thought that the fact that I wasn't born with psychic abilities and never had any magical experiences was a sign that I wasn't destined to become a magician. I realize now that I was wrong. I was born with a personality trait that compelled me to take a difficult programming course I wasn't required to take just to expand my horizons. In other words, I was born with a personality trait that compelled me to take on roles I had never taken on before. Looking back, I realize that the presence of this trait in my personality was a far better indicator that I would one day become a magician than being born with psychic abilities or having cool magical experiences before beginning my training would have been.

In the image of the Magician card shown at the beginning of IIH, the electric and magnetic fluids are represented symbolically by the sun and the moon, and their influence in the microcosm is represented symbolically by the red and blue colors permeating the figures of the man, woman, and hermaphrodite at the bottom. The message is clear. To become a magician, the electric and magnetic aspects of one's personality must both be developed equally and thoroughly. The electric aspect of one's personality is the part that pertains to, as Bill puts it, "independence, strength, courage, conviction, faith, will, determination, dedication, self-reliance, self-mastery, uprightness, clarity, order, adaptability, practicality, planning, productivity, excitement, exhilaration, creativity, and vision." The magnetic aspect of one's personality is the part that pertains to "peace, repose, calmness, happiness, contentment, serenity, tranquility, well-being, delight, kindness, gentleness, affection, empathy, tenderness, sensuality, pleasure, bliss, ecstasy, compassion, and love." This has nothing to do with physical sex or gender. Everyone's personality possesses some electric and some magnetic qualities. The idea is to develop and strengthen both types of qualities in oneself so they reinforce and support each other. In this way, one becomes a fully balanced and mature being.

In alchemy, the sun is the symbol of the electric aspect of the universe while the moon is the symbol of the magnetic aspect of the universe. Of the planetary symbols, those of Solar, Venus, and Mars indicate an electric nature, possessing the solar circle in their design. The planetary symbols of Luna, Jupiter, and Saturn indicate a magnetic nature, possessing the lunar crescent in their design. On the symbol of Mercury possesses both the solar circle and the lunar crescent. The Greek Hermes, who was analogous to the Roman Mercury, was seen as the archetype of all initiates. The Hermetic Order of the Golden Dawn attributed the planet Mercury to the Magician card. When it comes to what it means to be a magician, some interesting insights can be gained by studying Mercury and its correspondences.

The metal that corresponds with Mercury is mercury. Place a cube of iron in a bowl. It stays a cube. Place a cube of iron in a pan. Its form does not change. Now place mercury in a bowl, it then becomes the bowl. Similarly, if you place mercury in a pan, it takes on the form of a pan. It doesn't matter what you put mercury in. If you put it in a cup or flask, it becomes a cup or flask. If you put it in a mug or dish, it becomes a mug or dish. Mercury is not afraid to fill roles and does so easily. Be like mercury, my friend.

John O'Donohue writes the following in Anam Cara.

"In the western tradition, we were taught many things about the nature of negativity and the nature of sin, but

we were never told that one of the greatest sins is the unlived life. We are sent into the world to live to the full everything that awakens within us and everything that comes toward us. It is a lonely experience to be at the deathbed of someone who is full of regret to hear him say how he would love another year to do the things his heart had always dreamed of but believed he could never do until he retired."

The western esoteric tradition seems to have a fixation with death. One of the cards in the Major Arcana is called "Death". One of the texts that greatly influenced western magic is the *Egyptian Book of the Dead*. The process of exteriorizing one's subtle bodies is reminiscent of the process of dying. In some esoteric traditions, initiation is seen as the death of one's old self and the birth of one's new self.

This fixation with death is reflected in the general praxis of western magical traditions and systems. There are numerous exercises that involve passing through the death process while alive via the techniques of visionary magic. I can think of eight books off the top of my head that include an exercise of this nature. Those exercises have their value. An understanding of death will prove useful to any magician. However, it's important to remember that, at the end of the day, magic is "a way to discover and to make one's best choices in life." The magician should spend far more time studying life and engaging life than studying death. Imagine an actor who is given the option of performing on stage but decides not to because he would rather study the Egyptian Book of the Dead instead. I see a lot of actors like that in the esoteric community.

Chapter 12: Compassion

To be compassionate is to have an open heart. In the magical worldview, the heart and mind are connected. Therefore, opening one's mind facilitates the process of opening one's heart, and vice versa. On the Kabbalistic Tree of Life, an open heart is a virtue of Tiphereth while an open mind is a virtue of Hod. There is a path that connects Tiphereth and Hod. Once you reach Hod (obtain an open mind), it is very easy to reach Tiphereth (an open heart).

Because having an open mind is an important step in developing an open heart and acquiring the quality of compassion that arises from an open heart, I want to begin by discussing the concept of an open mind and the process of attaining one. In the Hod chapter of TRFSS(EV), Bill gives the following suggestion to those who wish to develop an open mind.

> *"Learn to argue both sides of any position with equal clarity and enthusiasm. Make this a lifelong ambition. That is, before you take a position, make sure you understand the strengths and weaknesses of opposing points of view."*

The first time I did this, it wasn't because I wanted to develop an open mind. It was because I was forced to. I was in grade school and a social studies teacher asked me to write an essay arguing that America succeeded in remaining neutral during WWI up until the point when it formally entered the war. I didn't agree with this position. I thought there were many actions taken by the American government that showed it clearly was not neutral. However, the essay prompt clearly told me to argue that America was neutral. And so, because the essay was a major part of my grade, I ended up writing a long essay to support a position I did not hold.

Later, in high school, I joined the speech and debate team. The type of debating I did was called "public forum debating (PF)." The issue to be debated at each tournament was decided upon ahead of time. My partner and I had to prepare arguments for both sides of the issue because we never knew which side we'd be asked to argue in support of during the tournament.

However, although these experiences forced me to look at both sides of various issues, they didn't teach me the importance of being able to look at both sides of an issue. Even after leaving the debate team, I still frequently made stupid decisions that seemed smart at the time. The reason being, I didn't realize that the stupid decisions were stupid because I didn't look at both sides of the issue.

Most people get angry when they encounter views that don't align with their own views. This is obvious if you go on social media. Most people on Facebook unfriend those whose views don't align well with theirs. If you see a comment on a post that reflects a view that doesn't align with your own views, you feel compelled to tell the commentator why he is wrong. I've had the good fortune of meeting several mature people over the course of my life, and one thing I notice about a lot of them is that they love talking to people with different views from them. It helps to expand and open their minds.

Levi tells us that "A man should form his opinions in freedom, and thus he may resemble the ideal of Divinity." Bill, similarly, tells us the following when it comes to trying to remain open-minded.

> *"Beware the super ego. The super ego is the socially accepted norms, attitudes, opinions, and conclusions that are assumed to be true. Check facts for yourself. Draw your own conclusions."*

The super ego is what prevents us from forming our opinions in freedom and, in this way, resembling the ideal of Divinity. It's what prevents us from looking at both sides of a position. We identify with our super egos and therefore can only view the world from the perspective of our super egos. This means that we can only understand and take the position of our super ego.

Bill further explains that practicing active listening will help you free yourself from your super ego. Active listening is a specific technique that is used in various forms of counseling and therapy. You actually don't even need active listening. You just need listening. However, true listening is more than just hearing.

In his book *The Lost Art of Listening*, Michael Nichols writes the following:

"Genuine listening means suspending memory, desire, and judgement—and, for a few moments at least, existing for the other person."

Memory, desire, and judgements are all components or functions of the super ego. This is another way of saying that you need to suspend the super ego in order to really listen. This statement pops up dozens of times in the book in slightly different wording. For example, he also writes that "the act of listening requires a submersion of the self and immersion in the other." The bottom line is that whenever you want to listen to someone, your super ego gets in the way of genuine understanding, and so in order to truly listen, you have to suspend the super ego. That is to say, you have to detach yourself from your super ego in such a way that it is no longer in your awareness, and then let the person you are listening to occupy the entirety of your awareness. This is why genuine listening frees you from your super ego.

For all of the aforementioned reasons, learning to listen will open your mind. It will also open your heart; that is to say, it will make you more compassionate. To truly listen to someone is indeed a compassionate act. As Michael Nichols states, "Being listened to means that we are taken seriously, that our ideas and feelings are known and, ultimately, that what we have to say matters." In other words, to listen to someone is to assert that they are worth listening to, and that this is because whatever part of themselves they are trying to express is valuable and meaningful.

Let's talk about the nature of unconditional compassionate love. No love emanates from a closed heart. Unconditional love emanates from an open heart. Conditional love emanates from a partially open heart.

Conditional love means you love people under certain conditions. For example, consider a member of an organized religion who loves all people who belong to the same religion as he does but hates all people who belong to a different religion. Basically, it means you love some people but not others, and that certain "conditions" determine whether or not you love any particular person.

Expressing conditional love is better than expressing no love at all; however, it's not good enough for those who intend to become adepts. The student of magic should strive to express unconditional love.

Part of loving a person is desiring the well-being of that person. If you love your mother, you want your mother to feel a sense of well-being. If you love your pet cat, you want your cat to feel a sense of well-being.

Your heart is open to those whom you love. It is closed to those whom you don't love. To have a fully open heart is to love everyone. To open your heart to those whom you don't love, you must learn to love them. In order to do this, you must act like you love them.

This is the principle behind one of the most potent spiritual exercises developed in western esotericism. Many masters and adepts from a variety of esoteric and magical systems have recommended this exercise to their students because it opens their hearts and furthers their spiritual development. This exercise is called "praying for your enemies" and is exactly what it sounds like. That said, I don't like the term "enemies" and therefore prefer to call this exercise "praying for those you dislike."

Take a moment to do just that. Pray for the well-being of someone you dislike. Maybe it's someone who bullied you in school, or a former boss who fired you for no reason whatsoever, or an ex who cheated on you, or a vandal who painted graffiti on your car. Pray for that person to have a life filled with joy and wonder.

There is an infinite ocean of compassionate love in your heart, yet hatred and animosity block a portion of this love and prevent it from flowing out to some people. When you pray for those you dislike, you are forcing the love in your heart through those barriers of hatred and animosity. This destroys those barriers.

In the esoteric world, you will meet many "adepts" who curse and hex those whom they dislike. They're not real adepts. The real adepts pray for those they dislike. The master Jesus Christ, one of the greatest magicians to walk this Earth, is a great example of someone who continually expresses unconditional love. One line of the Christmas carol "Hark the Herald Angels Sing" states regarding Christ that "Light and life to all he brings." Christ didn't just bring light and life to a few people whom he happened to like. He brought light and life to everyone because he loved everyone, regardless of who they were, or what they had done in the past, or what they were going to do in the future. His love was unconditional.

I think the enormous importance of compassionate love in magic is best reflected in these teachings of the master Jesus Christ, transmitted to us via the writings of his disciple Paul.

> *"If I speak in the tongues of men or of angels, but do not have love, I am only a resounding gong or a clanging cymbal. If I have the gift of prophecy and can fathom all mysteries and all knowledge, and if I have a faith that can move mountains, but do not have love, I am nothing."*

In the occult world, we find many people who have devoted hours of their lives studying what they were led to believe is the language of the angels. We find many people who practice divination because they want to "fathom all mysteries and all knowledge." We find many people who would desire to be able to move mountains with their magical power. However, we find few people who strive to learn how to love. In the eyes of an adept, the ability to speak the language of the angels, the ability to fathom all mysteries and all knowledge via divination, and the ability to move mountains through raw magical power are meaningless and insignificant if you do not know how to love.

Compassionate love corresponds with Tiphereth, which is the Sphere of the Sun. The sun is the source of life, and therefore, in a sense, compassion is about giving others life. That's a weird way of putting a relatively simple concept. Go back to the end of the previous chapter and reread the excerpt from *Anam Cara*. A large part of compassion is about helping people not end up like the person on the deathbed who is full of regret and wants another year to do the things he always wanted to do. Think about those closest to you. Ask yourself what you can do to prevent those people from becoming the regretful person on his deathbed.

Levi writes that "An imagination is not a realized thing; it is only a promised something, while an act is reality." I wrote extensively about compassion in my first book. When you read what I wrote, you probably imagined that you would strive to be more compassionate and to act more compassionately towards others. However, none of that will matter if you do not allow that which you imagined to manifest in the form of action.

I thought about telling you to close this book, think of one thing you can do to be a more compassionate person, and then to do that thing. Sometimes, you just have to get the ball rolling. I actually like that expression a lot. When I first thought of writing a book about the Six-Pronged Attack, I thought there was no way I could write enough to create a whole book. However, I sat down and started writing. I got the ball rolling and I very quickly found myself with a manuscript over 80,000 words long.

However, I'm not going to tell you to put down this book, think of something you can do in order to be a more compassionate person, and then go do it. If I didn't mention before, I love creative writing. I write short stories for fun and I hope to one day write novels. The process of writing out your life mirrors the process of writing out a story. When you begin to write a story, you don't decide upon a plot immediately. You brainstorm ideas. You come up with possibilities. Then, you narrow down those ideas and possibilities until finally you come up with a single coherent plot.

This kind of approach can also be used to write out the story of your life. Don't try to think of what you will do in the future. Think of several possible things you can do in the future. Then, analyze them and determine which one appeals to you the most.

So, close this book for a moment and think of five things you can do to become a more compassionate person. Then, pick one of these things and do it. Get the ball rolling.

Constructive Criticism

Being compassionate towards others doesn't always mean being nice towards others. It means doing what's best for others. You can be nice to a child by giving him whatever he wants whenever he wants it, but in the long run, this is going to be bad for the child because it's going to cause him to grow up to be a spoiled brat.

Therefore, being compassionate to someone doesn't mean you never criticize him. It just means that if you ever do criticize him, the criticism you give him is constructive criticism.

Constructive criticism is criticism that helps people improve themselves. Basically, when you give someone constructive criticism, you explain to him how he can improve himself but you word your explanation in a manner that is respectful and not hurtful.

In an ideal relationship, two lovers help each other improve. To do this, the lovers need to give each other constructive criticism.

Destructive criticism takes the form of insults, slander, condemnations, and nagging. It is inspired by malice. Constructive criticism, on the other hand, is inspired by compassion. You give someone constructive criticism to help them improve themselves.

I write both nonfiction and fiction. Both the nonfiction-writing and fiction-writing aspects of my being improve when I receive constructive criticism. For example, a friend of mine who was recently reading a short story of mine explained to me that I am not great at writing endings. She gave me specific reasons why I am not good at endings, and therefore, I learned specific things I could work on to improve my endings. I'm grateful to her for her constructive criticism because it helps me improve as a writer.

Again, I must reiterate the fact that constructive criticism is always worded in the least hurtful way possible. If you can reword a piece of criticism so that it's less hurtful, then it's destructive criticism, not constructive criticism.

Chapter 13: Melons

In *Anam Cara*, John O'Donohue tells a story about a king who doesn't like melons. One day, the king hears a knock on his door. It's an old man who wants to give him a melon as a gift. The same old man returns every day to give the king a new melon as a gift. Later, the king finds out that the melons aren't melons, but balls filled with jewels.

The meaning of this story is as follows. You are the king. The old man is life. The melons are unpleasant experiences. When life hands you unpleasant experiences, you don't appreciate them, after all, no one in their right mind likes unpleasant experiences. However, later on, you realize that such experiences are often extremely valuable in some way.

The introductory programming course I mentioned in Chapter 11 is an example of such an experience. The experience really sucked, and for a while, that's all I thought it was–an experience that sucked. Later, I realized that it really was actually as valuable as a big ball of jewels. These days, whenever something bad happens to me, I don't think "Aw man, something bad has happened to me." I think "Hey look, another ball of jewels disguised as a melon."

As another example of balls of jewels disguised as melons, let's consider a hypothetical situation where you are laid off from work. The day after you are laid off, the building you worked at collapses and everyone in it dies. Getting laid off was a ball of jewels disguised as a melon. If you reflect back on your own life, I'm sure you'll find many instances where you were given balls of jewels disguised as melons. This is an interesting subject; however, there is a related but different subject I think is far more interesting. In the story O'Donohue tells, imagine if the old man had given the king an object that could turn into a melon or a ball of jewels depending on what he did with it. That happens a lot too. Life will throw something into your path and what you do with it determines if it ultimately becomes a melon or a ball of jewels.

For example, I once had to live with a roommate who was extremely manipulative. He would constantly manipulate me into doing things I didn't want to do. Being stuck with this roommate was a big melon that life handed me, but it really did turn out to be a ball of jewels. I got so frustrated with the way he was successfully manipulating me to do things I didn't want to do that I began studying methods and technique for defending myself against manipulation. I ended up mastering those techniques in a short amount of time. Why was I able to master those techniques in a short amount of time? Well, since my roommate was constantly trying to manipulate me, I had many opportunities to practice using those techniques. As you can imagine, I got good at them real fast.

As you can see, life handed me a situation—being stuck with a manipulative roommate. I could have treated the situation as something to be passively suffered through. In this case, the situation would have been a melon. However, I treated the situation as an opportunity to practice defending myself against manipulation. For this reason, the situation ended up becoming a ball of jewels.

Look at the Yin Yang symbol. There's a black dot in the white region and a white dot in the black region. Nothing is ever completely black or completely white. Nothing in life is ever 100% a ball of jewels or 100% a melon. Even something that looks like it is just a melon is in part a ball of jewels. Or, to put it another way, every cloud has a silver lining. Sometimes, you have to find the part of a melon that is a ball of jewels—the part of the cloud that is the silver lining. You might think to yourself that it's so small that it isn't worth very much. Life is dynamic, as are all aspects of and situations in life. If you find the part of the melon that is the ball of jewels, you can tend to that part, nurture it, and cultivate it so that it grows bigger. For example, if a bad experience teaches you an important lesson, you can write down that lesson so you don't forget it, contemplate the lesson, and apply the lesson practically in order to further internalize it. Every bad experience is a learning experience. The sooner you realize that and make a conscious effort to discover what is to be learned from each new bad experience you undergo, the quicker you will become more mature.

And finally, let's not forget that alchemy exists. Just as the principles of alchemy can be used to transmute lead into gold, they can be used to transmute melons into balls of jewels.

Kurt Lewin, a famous psychologist, once said "If you want to truly understand something, try to change it." When you try to transmute a melon into a ball of jewels, you may eventually come to understand that it is already a ball of jewels, and that it was only your limited perception that caused you to see it as a melon.

Sometimes, life will hand you an object, and you will be convinced it is a melon. You won't believe there is any possible way for the object to be anything other than a melon, or for it to somehow be transmuted into a melon. For this reason I want to end this chapter with a discussion on, of all things, the rune Nauthiz. In his book *Teutonic Magic: The Magical and Spiritual Practices of the Germanic Peoples*, Kveldulf Gundarsson writes the following about the rune Nauthiz.

> *"Nauthiz is the testing and suffering which brings the hidden magical force of Fehu forth. It is the self-generated fire kindled in the time of greatest need."*

Fehu is the raw power of the magician. The truth is, we all possess enormous amounts of power deep within us. The trained magician can draw upon this power to perform miracles. However, drawing upon this power is a skill that needs to be learned. Concentration exercises, visualization exercises, and pore breathing exercises are part of the process of reawakening our innate ability to access power, but sometimes, more is needed. Sometimes, testing and suffering is needed. This kind of testing and suffering forces you to become aware of the inner strength you possess and to use this strength because if you do not, you will be destroyed.

Gundarsson continues as follows:

> *"This rune is the force of friction and resistance which builds up the individual strength and will. Its being is best written out in sayings, 'Every battle that doesn't kill you makes you strong,' and 'No pain, no gain.'"*

Gundarsson then points out that when the influence of Nauthiz permeates a person's life, "it may bring about hardships which teach that person an important lesson and ultimately strengthens her/him." These hardships will undoubtedly be viewed as melons by the person going through them until enough time has passed for the person to reflect back on their experience and realize that it provided with great strength. Near the end of his chapter on Nauthiz, Gundarson writes the following.

> *"Nauthiz develops both the will and the self-sufficiency of the vitki (magician). Its hardships must be faced with only your own might, and only the self-generated fire can overcome them. Nauthiz is the rune of trial and testing."*

Variants of the idea that there is a self-generated fire within you that is stoked by trial and testing (or in other words, there is a form of inner strength you possess that is augmented by trial and testing) appear in many places in magical literature. The Hebrew letter corresponding to the rune *Nauthiz* is Nun, which is also the first letter of *Netzach*. Regarding Netzach, Josephine writes that the essence of Netzach relates to victory, endurance, or victory through endurance. She further remarks that "the word Netzach, when used magically by a Jewish Kabbalist, will trigger a flow of power into the life of the person that will teach him or her the wisdom that strength comes from endurance. It will literally trigger situations around the person that gives the opportunity to grow strong through constant struggle." Again, that constant struggle is just going to seem like a giant melon until many years have passed and you look back and realize that it was actually a giant ball of jewels.

And in PITSOM V, Bill writes the following:

"In the books written by Carlos Castaneda, the Yaqui sorcerer Don Juan said that in order to face the unknown, the Nagual, a young apprentice often must undergo servitude to a petite dictator. The petite dictator is anyone who tries to totally dominate others and subject them to his will. In fighting to be free of this dominating individual, a student of magic learns to develop his own will power. He is witness to power in its negative aspect and must in turn exert tremendous will in a positive way to overcome it. But this is not just about developing one's will power and distinguishing positive from negative. It is about a requirement necessary for facing the unknown. To face the unknown, a student needs to be bring all the resources of his being into play in order to overcome an obstacle. Similarly, to enter the divine world, you need to have total will power and conviction at your disposal so as not to rely upon the support of society and the rules relating to custom and conformity."

There it is again. That "total power and conviction" Bill writes about is represented by the rune Fehu referenced in the first quote from Gundarsson I presented. Also, in fighting to be free from the petite dictator, the Nagual strives to obtain the "victory through endurance" that Josephine mentioned. Needless to say, the presence of a petite dictator in your life is also going to seem like a melon in your life. If you just passively suffer at the hands of the petite dictator and accept your fate, then the petite dictator will in fact be a melon and nothing more than a melon. However, if you struggle to overcome the negative form of power embodied by the petite dictator and, out of necessity, discover the presence of the Fehu power within you, then you will achieve the victory through endurance represented by Netzach and you will find that the petite dictator was really a ball of jewels.

Chapter 14: A Few More Things

Think of the process of becoming more mature as a puzzle that we're trying to piece together. In this chapter, I present four more pieces of the puzzle so we can have a more complete picture of what it takes to be mature. I begin by discussing conscience because acting maturely often means acting ethically, and your conscience is what tells you whether or not something is ethical. I then discuss the importance of making Second Circle your default state because the First Circle state of the insecure and the Third Circle state of bullies are usually not conducive to mature behavior. I then discuss the importance of being immune to the effects of insults and flattery instead of being easily influenced by insults and flattery like an immature person. Finally, I discuss the importance of possessing self-appreciation because this is something every healthy functional adult should have.

Conscience

"Our conscience is the voice of our Holy Guardian Angel, speaking to us in every moment of our existence. It never misleads. It is the clarity of the Self, flowing into us, seeking expression. All we need to do is trust it and obey it."

~Rawn Clark

The issue of ethics and morality in magic is one that is frequently discussed and debated in the esoteric community. However, when it comes to genuine magic, the issue of how to act morally/ethically is really quite simple.

Whenever you are confronted with a moral/ethical dilemma, listen to your conscience. Your conscience, also known as your "moral compass," always points in the right direction. There's a good chance you'll be faced with a moral/ethical dilemma at some point in your magical career. Again, whenever this happens, just listen to your conscience.

Do not fall into the trap of rationalization.[18] When you are tempted to perform an unethical action and your conscience tells you that the action is unethical, it is very easy to think of logical reasons why the action actually isn't unethical. Essentially, you are trying to use logic to prove that your conscience is wrong and then acting in accordance with logic instead of in accordance with your conscience. In *The Magus of Strovolos*, Daskalos tells one visitor "You are too wedded to logic." Logic isn't bad. It's a very useful tool. However, supposedly-logical thinking is very easily influenced by biases. Furthermore, we should not attribute so much importance to logic that we no longer appreciate the importance of "illogical" things like faith, intuition, and everything that exists at a level higher than the mental plane.

Your moral compass is not a logical device. It's an intuitive device. One day I left my apartment to go buy some bottled water from a shop down the street. My intuition told me to take some cash with me. I usually didn't take cash with me because I knew the shop accepted a wide variety of credit cards. It turned out that there was something wrong with the cash register that day so they were only accepting cash for purchases. There was no way for logic and reason to tell me that I needed cash. However, my intuition was able to tell me I needed cash. As far as methods of acquiring knowledge go, intuition is superior to logic. Therefore, when it comes to knowing what is or isn't ethical, listen to your conscience.

Rawn also writes the following about one's conscience (moral compass):

> *"A person who has not achieved the elemental equilibrium bases their morals upon external input– from their parents, loved ones, church, society in general, etc. But the equilibrated individual bases their morality upon inner directives alone."*

To have an elemental equilibrium is to stand at the center of the Cross of Equilibrated Forces. Each of the cross's four arms corresponds to an element. The center corresponds to akasha, which is the source of the four elements. Akasha is the medium through which the will of Divine Providence is connected to the created universe. It is through akasha that you access Divinity, and therefore, it is through akasha that you can hear the voice of divine beings such as your Holy Guardian Angel. The closer you are to the central point, the more easily you can hear the voice of Divinity emanating from that point and guiding you as you seek to differentiate between right and wrong.

One thing to note about your conscience is that the more you ignore it, the less easily you can hear it the next time you need it. Thus, if you constantly ignore your conscience, you will eventually be wholly unable to hear your conscience. The screen of your moral compass will be clouded and you won't be able to see in what direction the needle is pointing. The dangers of ignoring your conscience are dire. Learn to listen to it, and then always listen to it.

The Second Circle

By this point in time, enough Bardonists have heard of and studied Patsy Rodenburg's book *The Second Circle* that most of what I write in this section will seem like common knowledge in the Bardon community. However, if you haven't heard of Rodenburg's book, this section was written for you.

Study Rodenburg's book and apply the knowledge contained within it. You'll probably end up working through IIH in half of the time you otherwise would have.

Part of magical training in the Bardon system is learning to be constantly present-minded. It's easier to be present-minded if you're in Second circle.

A big part of magical training centers on exploring the five senses. There's a chapter about using a Second Circle state to more thoroughly explore each of the five senses in Rodenburg's book.

Compassion and empathy are traits that are crucial in magic. It's easier to treat people with compassion and empathy if you are in Second Circle with them.

In Chapter 7, I discussed well-being. Needless to say, you will experience a greater sense of well-being if you are in Second Circle. If you are always in First Circle, you are more likely to be bullied and to feel insecure. If you are always in Third Circle, the tension inside of you will have negative effects on your health.

The magician should strive to stay healthy. The healthier you are, the easier of a time you will have in anything you do, magical or mundane. Josephine remarks in *Magical Knowledge II* that "you last a long longer and look good for a much longer time if you listen, respond, and care for your body." To truly listen to your body, you need to be in Second Circle with your body. Caring for your body often means keeping your body in Second Circle. Recall Rodenburg's remark that the Second Circle body is the one most suited to survive in the wilderness, which is humanity's natural domain. This is because the Second Circle body is fit, and therefore able to do things like escape from predators, catch food, etc.

Finally, the concept of fear and the process of dealing with one's fears are important subjects in magic.[19] Rodenburg provides a chapter on dealing with your fears in her book. It contains many useful insights.

Resh

In the introduction to *Dogma et Ritual de la Hautie Magie* and in the twentieth chapter of *The Magical Ritual of the Sanctum Regnum*, Eliphas Levi lists a number of powers and abilities supposedly possessed by the true magician He associates each of these powers/abilities with one of the Hebrew letters. The ability he associates with Resh is as follows:

"Never to feel love or hatred unless it is designed."

Out of all the powers/abilities Levi lists, this is probably the least incredible or dramatic. It's probably not surprising that I think this is one of the first abilities students of magic should begin contemplating and developing. When you're close to adepthood, you can worry about stuff like seeing God and communing with the Seven Genii around the throne (Aleph), making the Philosopher's Stone (Cheth), and controlling the weather (Tau). However, right at the beginning of your training, you should begin acquiring the ability associated with Resh.

At first, the Resh ability seems really weird. The adept, after all, should always feel unconditional compassionate love towards anyone. That's one of the defining features of an adept. As for hatred, an adept should never feel hatred. You become an adept halfway through the work of PME. Rooting out the personality traits that cause you to feel emotions like hatred occurs in Step 2, which is at the beginning of IIH.

The ability Levi associated with Resh is very important. However, because of the wording he used, it's just not explained well. Fortunately, in a passage elsewhere in his writings, he elaborates on this ability and explains it more clearly. Basically, a better way of describing the ability (using an affirmation instead of infinitives) is as follows:

> *"I will not allow negative feelings that arise from being criticized/insulted or positive feelings that arise from being flattered to control my decisions and actions."*

So, someone might insult you and this might cause you to feel hatred towards him. This hatred might cause you to do something you regret like punch him and get arrested as a result. Or, someone might flatter you and this might cause you to feel "love" for the person flattering you. This "love" might make you want to do favors for the flatterer, which would make it easy for the flatterer to take advantage of you.

So, when someone criticizes, condemns, mocks, ridicules, or insults you, do not allow the negative feelings that arise within you (e.g. anger, hatred, etc.) to compel you to act in an unwise manner. When someone flatters you, you're probably going to take a liking to the person who flatters you. That's just human nature. However, don't let being flattered cause you to act in an unwise manner. This is essentially what the Resh ability is all about.

Sit back and imagine someone who does not possess the Resh ability. When anyone criticizes him, he overreacts and throws a tantrum. When anyone flatters him, he feels very happy and showers the flatterer with favors. There's a good chance you're imagining a child because that's how immature people behave and many children are immature. If you walk up to Bill and call him an idiot, he's not going to give a shit. If you walk up to a toddler and call him an idiot, he's going to start crying. It's fine for toddlers to be like that. They're toddlers. They're not supposed to be super-mature. The problem is that there are leaders with enormous amounts of power who possess the same level of maturity. For example, there are presidents who arrest their countries' citizens for making Facebook posts critical of them. If you watch *Last Week Tonight with John Oliver*, you probably know the names of a few such presidents; after all, he does like to poke fun at them. Of course in the esoteric world we have people like Jake, who I mentioned in Chapter 2.

The idea of not allowing negative emotions to arise within you or influence your actions when you have been criticized, insulted, or attacked in some way is rather prevalent in the collective spiritual teachings of humanity. Jesus tells us to turn the other cheek rather than become hateful and express your hatred toward your assailant by slapping him back. There is also the story of Hazrat Ali, who refrained from killing an enemy on the battlefield when he was angry because he knew that there was great spiritual danger in letting anger influence your actions.[20] Swami Sivananda also repeatedly reminded his students that, when criticized/insulted, they have no reason to become angry because such criticism/insult does not affect and is meaningless to its target's true self (atman). So yeah, if you're criticized/insulted, don't react out of anger. Let reason, rational thinking, and wisdom determine the way you handle the situation. When it comes to being a spiritual, righteous, and mature person, this is pretty basic stuff.

The other half of the Resh power, on the other hand, isn't discussed nearly as much. However, it is just as important. When people flatter you, don't let any resulting positive emotions you feel towards the flatterer open you up to being taken advantage of by the flatterer. This whole idea of defending yourself against flattery is one I find very fascinating. Consider the following passage from Manuel Smith's book *When I Say No, I Feel Guilty*.

> *"If, on the other hand, we are independently assertive in our thoughts, feelings, and behavior, we reserve the final judgement of actions, even the positive ones, to ourselves. Such an assertive attitude does not make you loath to accept compliments and praise, but only to be the ultimate judge of the accuracy of such praise. For example, when you are genuinely complimented on your choice of clothes and you feel they suit you well, you might reply "Thank you. I think it looks nice too." On the other hand, when you suspect manipulative flattery, you might respond "Really, I don't understand. What is it about my clothes makes me look so good?"*

If I were to create a reading list of books I think are useful to the Bardonists, Manuel Smith's book would be near the top of the list. Part of magical training in the Bardon system involves establishing an elemental equilibrium. This means that you develop the fiery, airy, watery, and earthy aspects of your personality. Assertiveness is an important fiery trait, and therefore, developing assertiveness is an important part of developing the fiery aspect of your personality. Manuel Smith's book is one of the best guides to becoming assertive I know of. For the Bardonist on Step 2, this book is over a thousand times more valuable and useful than any book about ritual magic, sacred geometry, runes, or

Tantra could possibly be. Let's go back to the Resh power/ability, or rather my wording of it. Here it is again.

> *"I will not allow negative feelings that arise from being criticized or positive feelings that arise from being flattered to control my decisions and actions."*

Manuel Smith's book is in many ways 300-page guide to developing this ability. Through the techniques of fogging, negative assertion, and negative inquiry, you can defend yourself from insults, criticisms, and condemnations, without becoming angry in the process. Furthermore, by applying the assertive principles Smith teaches, you can also defend yourself against manipulative flattery. At the end of the day, those who insult you and those who flatter you are trying to manipulate you. The Resh ability is about becoming immune to manipulation. Remember, whoever controls your emotions controls you. If someone can cause you to feel hatred by insulting you or cause you to feel "love" by flattering you, then that person has control over your emotions, and therefore control over you. Part of being assertive is asserting that you are the only one in control over your emotions and the only one with the right to control your emotions.

Self-Appreciation

The subject of magical protection is one that pops up a lot in the esoteric world. Over the course of the last century, many rituals, spells, and other magical techniques have been developed for blocking curses, banishing demons, and removing negative energy from rooms or objects. However, the process of learning magical self-defense doesn't begin with learning those rituals, spells, and magical techniques. It begins with acquiring self-appreciation. In his essay on the lunar spirit Emvatibe, Bill writes the following.

> *"Many times negative energy can only influence us if it has some kind of hook or tie to us. It uses our own errors and weaknesses of character to infiltrate and weaken our will. But if you have a really healthy self-appreciation and cherish all the good that has happened to you in life, then you do not open yourself up to receive the negative. You sense its nature early on and simply turn away from it. You realize it is not part of yourself and that you wish to have nothing to do with it."*

A study of psychology will show just how much of a negative impact a lack of self-appreciation will have on your life. According to Michael Nichols, how well you can appreciate others depends on how well you can appreciate yourself. If you don't appreciate yourself, you're less likely to appreciate others, and therefore more likely to do things that make your loved ones feel unappreciated and insignificant.

To lack self-appreciation is to be insecure. Insecurities prevent us from listening. They cause us to overreact and to misinterpret the statements and actions of others. They lead to us being paranoid and unnecessarily suspicious. The events that prevent us from feeling self-appreciation often occur during our childhood. So long as you don't feel self-appreciation, you allow those events to control you. This means that to some extent, you are still trapped in your childhood. To become mature, you need to grow past those events and overcome the negative impact they have on your present. This means you need to develop self-appreciation.

In Step 1, you create your soul mirrors. While creating your black soul mirror, it is easy to lose your appreciation for yourself. In fact, some Bardonists even advise you to take a hostile attitude toward yourself when making your black soul mirror. This is bad advice. At no point in your training should you lose your self-appreciation. If you lack self-appreciation, you need to find a way to develop self-appreciation or you won't get very far.

If you don't have self-appreciation and someone tells you that you suck, that insult is going to cut very deep into you because it confirms something you already suspect. You're likely to overreact to such a statement and respond with aggression. Your lack of self-appreciation has caused you to be open to the insult and to receive it into you. This has allowed the insult to influence you and hook you into acting in a negative manner. However, if you possess self-appreciation, then when someone tells you that you suck, you can just laugh at the comment and shrug it off. This is just one example of how self-appreciation can protect you from the kind of negativity from insecure people. A healthy self-appreciation protects you from all kinds of negativity, both magical and mundane.

Chapter 15: Wisdom

There are literally volumes of books written about what wisdom is and isn't by a variety of philosophers, many of whom vehemently disagree with each other. I'm trying to keep this book both as practical as possible and as concise as possible because I am writing for students of magic, not philosophy. For this reason, I have refrained from making this chapter unnecessarily lengthy. Wisdom may be profound, but the methods and approaches to the process of acquiring it can be summarized in a simple and concise manner.

What is Wisdom?

In *The Spirit of Magic,* I defined wisdom as follows:

"Wisdom is the ability to know the will of Divine Providence."

That's a pretty accurate definition of wisdom. However, it's not the only possible way to define wisdom. When it comes to understanding a profound concept like wisdom, it often helps to view the concept from different angles. These different angles can be summarized in different definitions. In PITSOM I, Bill writes "I think of magic as a way to discover and to make one's best choices in life." Consider the following definition of wisdom.

"Wisdom is the ability to know what the best choices in life are."

Is this definition the same as previous one about knowing the will of Divine Providence? I think they are, although some people might find it difficult to see how this is so. Consider this. Do you think it's the will of Divine Providence that you don't make the best choices in life? Divine Providence is infinitely compassionate.

She wants only the best for us, and that is the same as saying she wants us to make the best choices in life. However, don't get me wrong. Making the best choices in life doesn't just mean you make the choices that will get you an easy life. It often means making choices that will cause you to overcome challenges in order to transform the world in significant ways because by doing so, you will become something far greater than you can ever imagine at your present stage of evolution.

Goethe once said "Knowing is not enough; we must apply." The veracity of this statement asserts itself numerous times throughout your magical training. For example, in the Step 1 astral work, you make your soul mirrors and, as a result, know the ways you are unbalanced. In the Step 2 astral work, you apply this knowledge as you work to bring yourself into a state of balance.

It's great to know the will of Divine Providence or to know what the best choices in life are, but you won't be any better off if you don't apply this knowledge. Sometimes it's hard to make the best choice, even if you know what the best choice is. Temptation can still compel you to make the wrong choice. This is why it's also essential to develop qualities like self-discipline in addition to wisdom. So, acquiring wisdom is not the entirety of the magician's spiritual development. However, it is a key component of the magician's spiritual development.

Why TRFSS(EV) is a Treasure to the Magical Community

Go back to the Malkuth chapter of TRFSS(EV). At the very beginning of that chapter, Bill writes the following.

> *"If you are here in this world wearing a human body, then the prime directive that overrides all other considerations is that you are free to choose for yourself what you wish to do with your life. Other considerations may weigh heavily upon you, but in the end, it is your life to live.*

> *But to actually discover for yourself your best choices in life? Well, that may take you on a journey through all the sephiroth."*

Let's examine this passage, because I believe it is the key to understanding the entirety of TRFSS(EV).

Malkuth is the sephirah of our physical mundane day-to-day lives. In this passage, Bill reveals that everyone who incarnates in Malkuth is given a task, and that this task is "to choose for yourself what you wish to do with your life." Of course, we could just say to ourselves "Great, I'll go do that," and then forget about the other sephiroth. The thing is, your path in life (what you do with your life) is determined by your choices, and to live the best life, you need to make the best choices. To do that, you need wisdom; after all, wisdom is by definition the ability to know the best choices in life. Bill further states that striving to acquire this wisdom "may take you on a journey through all the sephiroth." Each of the sephiroth past Malkuth contains a bit of wisdom that will guide you as you achieve the prime directive of Malkuth—the directive to "choose for yourself what you wish to do with your life."

When it comes to developing wisdom, we need to use a multi-pronged approach. Of course, establishing an elemental equilibrium will help us become wise because, as pointed out in the previous chapter, it puts us in communion with akasha and therefore with Divinity, which allows us to hear the voice of Divinity better. However, as far as establishing wisdom goes, you'd also do well to study TRFSS(EV) a lot. The whole essay is about wisdom—different aspects of wisdom categorized by the sephiroth.

Wisdom According to Bardon

In IIH, Bardon writes that "wisdom does not depend on mind and memory but on the maturity, purity and perfection of the individual personality." This means that wisdom doesn't depend on how smart you are or on how much knowledge you have stored away in your mind. Being smart and having a lot of knowledge are useful traits, but they don't necessarily make someone wise. Wisdom depends on maturity. It also depends on the purity and perfection of the individual personality. Purity just refers to how pure the personality is. "Perfection" refers to how balanced the personality is. Bardon is saying that the more pure and balanced your personality is, the wiser you will be. Of course, having a pure and balanced personality is synonymous with having an elemental equilibrium.

Wisdom via Understanding

In Kabbalah, wisdom pertains to the sephirah Chockmah, while understanding pertains to the sephirah Binah. Chockmah and Binah were created at the same time. One cannot exist without the other. This means that if you have wisdom, then you also have understanding. It also means that if you have understanding, then you also have wisdom. Many people are accustomed to thinking that Chockmah is the second sephirah and Binah is the third sephirah and that this means Chockmah came before Binah. However, both Chockmah and Binah reside above the abyss, and therefore outside of time. They are the opposite ends of polarized Divinity. When you create the idea of "big," you simultaneously create the idea of "small." When you create the idea of "long," you simultaneously create the idea of "short." Similarly, when Chockmah came into being, Binah came into being simultaneously because Chockmah just can't exist without Binah.

If you acquire understanding, you will acquire wisdom because wisdom and understanding are always found together. Therefore, to acquire wisdom, strive to acquire understanding. The process of acquiring understanding begins with understanding the microcosm—yourself. This is done by creating the soul mirrors, studying your soul mirrors, and constantly introspecting and retrospecting while recording one's findings.

Wisdom via Compassion

In Kabbalah, it is taught that Chockmah and Binah give birth to Tiphereth. Since Tiphereth is the sephirah of compassion, this means that acquiring wisdom and understanding will lead to one acting compassionately. In other words, wise people act compassionately.

It's a well-known principle, at least in the Bardon system, that if you want to develop a positive trait, you need to act as if you already possess that trait. For example, if you want to become a patient person, you need to act like a patient person. This is the so-called "volition prong" in the Six-Pronged Attack. It's called that because if often takes willpower to force yourself to act like you have the trait. If you're an impatient person and someone irritates you, then acting patiently does require a great deal of willpower in order to restrain yourself from lashing out.

From this principle, it's clear that if you want to become wise, one way to do this is to act like a wise person. Because wise people are compassionate, this means you should act compassionately towards others.

Three More Ways to Acquire Wisdom

There are several more ways one can acquire wisdom. Three of them are to reflect on your experiences, to assimilate wisdom from others, and to receive wisdom from Divinity by praying for it.

Your experiences provide you with wisdom. The more you reflect on your experiences, the more you learn from them and the wiser you become because of them. Failures are not always melons. They can be balls of jewels because they provide us with wisdom. Oftentimes, they can provide us with far more wisdom than successes can.

We can also acquire wisdom from wise people. One way to do this is by having conversations with wise people. After such conversations, it's often a good idea to write down what you've learned. Another way acquire wisdom from wise people is by reading their writings. *The Last Lecture,* by Randy Pausch, contains a lot of the author's wisdom. We can also look at more ancient texts—the *Book of Proverbs,* the Delphic maxims, the *Tao Te Ching,* etc.

Finally, you can pray for wisdom.

The Wisdom Rosary

As a fun project, consider making a wisdom rosary. Collect together a number of wisdom-themed prayers you can use. Decide on some numbers associated with wisdom that you can use, perhaps relating to the gematria of Hebrew words relating to wisdom. Then, with these prayers and numbers, design your rosary and make it.

I never got around to designing a customized wisdom rosary, but that's because a standard rosary works just fine for me. On the big beads, I pray my own variation of the prayer of St. Francis. On the small beads, I pray the following prayer:[21]

"Lord God Almighty, Creator and Maker of Heaven and Earth, please give me wisdom and understanding, and please help me become more compassionate. Amen."

You can also use your Bardonian mala. Pray the prayer above ten times at various points throughout the day. Use the mala to count. When you pray, make sure to stay present-minded and to mean what you say. Know that Divine Providence is listening. Speak with reverence. This isn't really the place to get into the nuances of correct prayer technique, but do know that mindlessly repeating a prayer you don't mean won't do you any good.

The *Ars Notoria* has several prayers for wisdom. Reading over them can give you ideas on composing your own prayers for wisdom. There are also a few psalms in the *Book of Psalms* that deal with wisdom. I don't like long prayers. I like short simple prayers that I can repeat over and over again using a rosary. That's just how I like to pray. However, when it comes to praying for wisdom, you need to find the approach that works best for you.

Chapter 16: Reading

Reading is an important part of the paths of most modern students of magic. In this chapter, I discuss my philosophy when it comes to reading. This chapter is divided into three sections. The first section concerns reading esoteric writings. The second, concerns reading non-esoteric nonfiction writings. The third concerns reading literary fiction.

Reading Esoteric Works

It might seem like I have something against reading esoteric writings. After all, I appear to always be telling people that there are more productive things to do than to read magical books.

In truth, I don't have anything against reading esoteric writings any more than I have anything against eating. However, I do think the way most students of magic approach the process of reading esoteric writings is less than ideal.

In Robert Ambelain's book *Spiritual Alchemy*, he discusses the seven deadly sins. These are lust, pride, anger, envy, sloth, gluttony, and avarice. Traditionally, gluttony refers to a tendency to consume too much food. However, Ambelain's book is written for students of esotericism. Therefore, in his book, Ambelain addresses a different kind of gluttony that he thinks poses more of a danger for students of esotericism when it comes to their spiritual evolution and advancement. The gluttony Ambelain discusses does not concern consuming too much food, but too many esoteric books.

That analogy is great. When it comes to reading esoteric books, I'm not saying you shouldn't do it at all. Just as a human being needs to consume food in order to grow, the student of esotericism needs to consume esoteric writings in order to grow. However, you shouldn't be a glutton when you do this.

Overeating is unhealthy. Similarly, over-consuming esoteric writings can be bad.[22] Most esoteric teachers will tell you that γνῶθι σεαυτόν was written over the front door of the Temple of

Apollo at Delphi.[23] Fewer esoteric teachers will tell you that μηδέν ἄγαν was also carved there.[24] That's unfortunate, because this second maxim is also very important. It certainly applies to the consumption of esoteric writings.

When it comes to food, there's a lot of junk food out there. Eating junk food is bad for you. Similarly, consuming junk esoteric writings can be bad for you. That's why you shouldn't consume too much of it.

Overeating healthy gourmet food is slightly better for your health than overeating junk food, but it's still unhealthy. So, don't do that. Eat the right amount of healthy gourmet food at any one sitting. The exact amount will depend on what you are eating, as well as on the capacity of your stomach.

When it comes to your magical advancement, you want to consume healthy gourmet magical writings. However, you don't want to be a glutton when doing this. Consume the right amount at any one sitting. The right amount depends on what exactly you are reading and what the capacity of your mind is. In other words, it depends on how much information you can comfortably and effectively assimilate before you suffer from an information overload.

Many years ago, I sat down at my computer and read the entirety of PITSOM IV in one sitting. That was a bad idea. It was too much for me to fully assimilate, so I was only able to retain a small portion of the knowledge contained in that essay. When some time had passed, I read through the essay again section by section over a period of several days. I learned a lot and benefitted greatly from it.

What is healthy gourmet food to you may be junk food to another. For example, the writings of Aleister Crowley are all healthy gourmet food to Thelemites. For Bardonists, they are ok food at best. Similarly, the essays in the PITSOM series are the pinnacle of healthy gourmet food for Bardonists, but for all I know, they could be junk food for Thelemites.

Balance is an important theme in magic. The magician should strive to approach all aspects of his life and his magical training in a balanced manner. You should strive to consume healthy foods, but don't eat the same healthy food all the time. Your diet will be unbalanced. William Mistele's writings are all healthy food, but don't consume his writings exclusively. Consume some stuff by Rawn Clark, Daskalos, Swami Sivananda, John O'Donohue, and other writers who were genuine magicians or spiritual teachers with a true connection to Divinity.

So in a nutshell, that's my philosophy towards reading esoteric works. Eat healthy. That means the following three things:

1. Eat nutritious food.
2. Eat a balanced diet.
3. Don't overeat (don't be a glutton).

Reading Non-Esoteric Non-Fiction

In Step 2, you work on establishing an elemental equilibrium. This involves developing the personality traits you need to develop in order to have a balanced personality. In Chapter 14, I mentioned Manuel Smith's book *When I Say No, I Feel Guilty*. I further remarked that for a person on Step 2, this book is more valuable than a thousand books on occult and esoteric subjects. I wasn't exaggerating. Honestly, if you were to ask me for a list of all the books I've ever read and to order this list by how much they helped me in my magical training, Manuel Smith's book would be much higher on the list than any books by the iconic figures in the history of western esotericism. So would *The Lost Art of Listening*, by Michael Nichols.

Consider a Bardonist at Step 2 who is reading a book about Enochian magic. If this Bardonist is reading the book for pleasure, then that's fine. If she is reading the book in hopes that she will find knowledge in it that will help her move on to Step 3, she is very misguided. You don't need to learn Enochian magic to move on to Step 3. However, if you are not assertive, you do need to become assertive to move on to Step 3. If you are not a good listener, you do need to become a good listener to move on to Step 3.

For any personality trait you wish to develop, there are many good resources that will help you develop that trait. Take the YouTube channel *Charisma on Command*, which is run by Charlie Houpert and Ben Altman. Many of their videos center on helping people become charismatic. If you're on Step 2 and you're socially awkward, or shy, or lack charisma in some way, then watching their videos is a much better use of your time than reading *Magick in Theory and Practice*. It's certainly not my intent to knock *Magick in Theory and Practice*. The book is useful for a certain set of people. Most Bardonists working through Step 2 are not in that set.

If you're on Step 2, you should be trying to eliminate your negative traits one by one. Do some research and try to determine if there's a good book that can help you eliminate the negative trait you are currently working on. There's a good chance there is, and there's a good chance it's more valuable to you at your current stage of advancement than most esoteric or spiritual books are.

There are many Bardonists who try to create resources for other Bardonists. For example, Rawn and Bill both have their sites filled with articles and essays. At the present, I think the most useful resource for Bardonists that could be created is a list of personality traits, each accompanied by a list of good resources to aid in their development. Only include resources that you yourself have used to and found to be valuable. For example, don't list every book about developing leadership under the leadership trait. Some of those books are good. Others aren't. If you read a book about leadership and find that it did indeed do a lot to help you become a better leader, add the book to the list so other Bardonists at Step 2 who need to become better leaders in order to establish an elemental equilibrium will know that they can benefit from the book. If the book did very little to help you become a better leader, don't add the book to the list.

Reading Literary Fiction

We gain wisdom and become mature by undergoing experiences that make us mature and provide us with wisdom. I've said that a million times in this book.

I was at a talk by Richard Russo about two weeks ago and during this talk he discussed a novel he wrote that was about parental anxiety. He mentioned that he strived to write well enough that those who read the novel also experienced the parental anxiety experienced by the novel's characters. He further remarked that this experience of parental anxiety was his gift to readers.

I thought that was an interesting concept. If you asked most people if they would consider the experience of parental anxiety to be a gift, they would look at you like you were crazy.

The phenomenon Russo alludes to is called "experience-taking." The basic idea is that when you read fiction, you undergo the experiences the characters you read about undergo. The power of the human imagination can do amazing things. Experiences change you. Studies have shown that experience-taking changes you in the same way. You change as if you yourself went through the experiences of the characters.

In my first book, *The Spirit of Magic*, I urged you all to read John Steinbeck's book *East of Eden*. Several of the characters in that book undergo experiences that make them more mature. When you read that book, the phenomenon of experience-taking allows you to undergo those same experiences, and to be more mature as a result.

Even if the phenomenon of experience-taking didn't exist, reading literary fiction would still be a productive use of your time. That's because a lot of literary fiction explores the theme of maturity, or some aspect of maturity. Therefore, reading literary fiction can help you develop a better understanding of maturity or of aspects of maturity. In *The Spirit of Magic*, I also mentioned T. Greenwood's book *This Shining World*, which explores the theme of responsibility. Becoming responsible is a part of becoming mature.

If you're looking for a good book for the purpose of undergoing experiences via experience-taking, I recommend Jennifer Eagan's *A Visit from the Goon Squad*. Each chapter in the book is told from a different character's point of view and centers on one of the most intense experiences of the character's life.[25]

Chapter 17: Charisma

I

Without a doubt, a chapter on charisma may seem out of place in a book about maturity. If I were to ask you to imagine someone who is mature, the person you imagine would probably be responsible, wise, compassionate, respectful, and open-minded, after all, these are traits that everyone associates with maturity. Indeed, how responsible, wise, compassionate, respectful, or open-minded someone is can be a very accurate indicator of how mature they are overall. For example, I don't know many irresponsible people who are mature, or many mature people who are irresponsible. Charisma isn't like that. Being charismatic doesn't make you mature. Despite this, charisma can be a useful tool that, if applied in the right way, will help you become more mature.

Part of maturity is being well-integrated into society. Charismatic people have an easier time integrating themselves into society than people who aren't charismatic. A lack of love during a person's childhood can have psychological effects that trap him in the past and prevent aspects of his development from moving forward (maturing). Dealing with these effects sometimes begins with ensuring that you don't continue to suffer from a lack of love. Charismatic people are more likely to be liked, appreciated, and acknowledged by others than uncharismatic people are.

In addition to all of this, other traits that are more directly related to maturity, such as confidence and the healthy self-appreciation discussed in Chapter 14, will become strengthened if you develop the trait of charisma because they are related to charisma.

II

In the previous section, I explained why charisma can be a tool to help you become more mature, even if being charismatic doesn't necessarily mean that you're mature. This book is about maturity, but it's also about magic. In light of this, I want to discuss the relationship between charisma and magic.

In one of his essays, Frater Acher writes the following about magic.

"The essence of magic is the ability to lead a happy life."

I really like this quote. I'm not sure if I agree with it one-hundred percent, but I do think it reflects an important truth. One of the results of your magical studies should be increased happiness in your life. I think having a charismatic personality is conducive to leading a happy life. You'll make more friends, relate better with others, and have more fulfilling social interactions if you're charismatic. Charisma will make you more successful. You actually see this principle reflected in disturbing ways sometimes. For example, sometimes if two people are running for a leadership position, the person who gets the most votes is the one who is the most charismatic instead of the one who is the most confident. I also know of at least one major court case in which the victor's efforts to be charismatic played a big role in their victory.[26]

III

I want to briefly explain what an aura is and clear up a few common misconceptions about them. Some people believe that the aura and the astra-mental body are the same. This is not true. Think about a magnet. A magnet is not a magnetic field. It is an object that produces a magnetic field. Your astra-mental body is like a magnet, and your aura is like the magnetic field around the magnetic. The nature of your astra-mental body determines the nature of your aura, but they are not the same.

IV

Magnets either attract each other or repel each other. Similarly, astra-mental bodies repel or attract each other. If your aura resonates well with others, it will attract them. This will make them inclined to like you and be friendly to you. The stronger your aura is, the stronger their inclination to like you is. In the case of people who are the opposite gender, they will be more inclined to fall in love with you if your aura resonates well with them. The stronger your aura is, the more inclined to fall in love with you they will be.

If you have an aura that resonates well with others and is very strong, you are said to be "charismatic."

V

Have you ever met someone and immediately disliked him, even though you just met and he has done nothing wrong to you. It's because your aura does not resonate well with his. Thus, they repel each other. If your aura doesn't resonate well with anyone else's, then everyone you meet will dislike you from the start. This will make life difficult. If you find yourself in this position, you need to change your aura so that it resonates well with others. If you do this, people will not be inclined to dislike you. If you change your aura so that it resonates well with others and strengthen your aura too, then others will be inclined to like you.

VI

Consider two people named Jack and Jill. If their auras resonate well with each other, then there will be an attractive force between them. If Jack's aura is much stronger than Jill's, then Jill will be attracted to Jack much more strongly than Jack will be attracted to Jill. If Jill's aura is much stronger than a Jack's, then Jack will be attracted to Jill much more strongly than Jill will be attracted to Jack.

If Jack and Jill's auras do not resonate well with each other, then there will be a repulsive force between them. If Jack's aura is much stronger than Jill's, then Jill will be repulsed by Jack much more strongly than Jack will be repulsed by Jill. If Jill's aura is much stronger than Jack's, then Jack will be repulsed by Jill much more strongly than Jill will be repulsed by Jack.

If your aura is weak, you will be attracted to those people whose auras resonate well with yours. If your aura is strong, those people whose auras resonate well with yours will be attracted to you.

VII

If you have an aura that doesn't resonate well with the auras of other people, you should transform yourself into the kind of person who has an aura that resonates well with others and then strengthen your aura so that people will be attracted to you. In other words, you should transform yourself into a charismatic person. There are two main ways to do this. The first way is to transform yourself from the inside out. The second way is to transform yourself from the outside in.

VIII

Transforming yourself into a charismatic person from the inside out is done through the use of conscious eating, conscious breathing, autosuggestion, and magical washing.

To use conscious eating, impregnate your food with charisma and eat it while believing with full conviction that you are consuming charisma. Do this at each meal.

To use conscious breathing, impregnate the air around you with charisma and breathe it in while believing with full conviction that you are inhaling charisma. Then, breathe out while believing with full conviction that you are exhaling shyness, social anxiety, social awkwardness, and all other traits you consider to be the opposite of charisma.

To use magical washing, turn the water cold while washing your hands or showering and feel the water pulling away from you shyness, social awkwardness, and any other traits that have a negative impact on your charisma.

To use autosuggestion, repeat the affirmation "I am charismatic" regularly, especially immediately before falling asleep and immediately after waking up.

After you have changed your aura so that it resonates well with others, you now need to strengthen your aura so that others will be attracted to you. In order to do this, you need to strengthen your astra-mental body; after all, this is what your aura emanates from. The strength of one's astra-mental body depends on the state of one's elemental equilibrium. The better your elemental equilibrium is, the stronger your astra-mental body will be, and therefore the stronger your aura will be.

IX

The procedure for becoming charismatic by transforming yourself from the outside in can be found in Patsy Rodenburg's book *The Second Circle*. The outermost level of your being is your actions. Thus, the outermost level of the physical aspect of your being is your physical actions. The outermost level of the astral aspect of your being is your astral actions; that is to say your feeling. The outermost level of the mental aspect of your being is your mental actions; that is to say your thinking. To change yourself into a charismatic person from the outside in, you begin by changing the outermost level of your being. This means you act like a charismatic person, feel like a charismatic person, and think like a charismatic person. Again, detailed instructions for doing this can be found in Rodenburg's book.

The YouTube channel Charisma on Command also has numerous great videos on changing yourself into a charismatic person from the outside in.

It is best to use both the outside in and inside out strategies simultaneously. In this way, you can be assured of success.

X

There is a third way to become charismatic. This is to start at the middle level of your being and to work simultaneously inward and outward until you have changed the entirety of your being so that it is charismatic. I don't know much about this way so I can't provide too many details or even complete instructions for using it. I can only give you some of its basic principles. Applying these principles may speed up your transformation into a charismatic individual.

The nature and strength of your aura are partially dependent on the nature and strength of the vitality (vital force) in your body. The third way centers on transforming your aura into a charismatic aura by working with your body's vitality.

The stronger your body's vitality is, the stronger your aura will be. If your aura doesn't resonate well with others, then this means that they will be more strongly repulsed by you. If your aura resonates well with others, then this means they will be more strongly attracted to you.

To strengthen your aura by strengthening your vitality, first stop doing those activities that deplete your vitality. Stop doing those activities that attract or create parasitical entities (such as larvae) that feed off your vitality. Strong negative feelings like anger, hatred, and fear can create or attract these entities. Consult the physical section of Step 6 of IIH for more information.

Make sure to eat fruits often. Fruits contain a lot of the life force of the plants they grow on, and thus, eating a lot of fruits can increase your body's natural vitality level.

Practice Bardon's vital force pore breathing techniques often. Remember that you must always pore breathe out the same amount of vital force that you pore breathe in. The idea here is not to accumulate a charge of vital force in your body. It is never a good idea to have an amount of vital force in your body that is greater than or less than your body's natural vitality level for an extended period of time. The idea is to flush out stagnant vitality and to replace it with fresh vitality. This also stretches and strengthens your etheric body, and will gradually increase your body's natural vitality level. However, increasing your body's natural vitality level is not the same as accumulating the vital force in your body and then leaving it there. Don't do that.

XI

In Bill's essay on the fire element, he writes the following:

> *"On the other hand, being obsessed, infatuated, or spellbound—these emotional states result in part from a weakness of the fire element within ourselves. We have failed to master the sources of power which animate our souls. Consequently, there are times when we may find ourselves attracted to experiences or people who are unfamiliar and yet strangely appealing. Captivating images may come to us in dreams or we may encounter ideals which bedazzle our imaginations."*

If your astra-mental body is weak, the aura emanating from your astra-mental body will be weak. This will cause you to become strongly attracted to those whose auras resonate well with yours. As Bill points out, it is possible to become so attracted to these people that you are obsessed and infatuated with them.

An imbalanced astra-mental body is a weak astra-mental body. Any kind of imbalance in your astra-mental body will make you prone to becoming infatuated with those whose auras are stronger than yours. According to Bill, an imbalance consisting of a weakness of the fire element makes you especially prone to becoming infatuated with those whose auras are strong than yours. If you find yourself infatuated with others, you will need to balance the elements in your astra-mental body. Consider beginning to work with the fiery aspect of your personality. Developing the trait of assertiveness is a great way to strengthen the fiery aspect of your personality. Manuel Smith's book is a great guide to developing that trait. Self-discipline is another important fire trait, so take advantage of opportunities to exercise self-discipline.

XII

Do not make the mistake of thinking you can balance, purify, and refine the fiery aspect of your personality by doing fire meditations and exercises. Before you have established an elemental equilibrium, any meditative or magical work with fire will unbalance you further and exacerbate the problems in your personality relating to the fire element.

Eliminate your negative fire traits. Develop positive fire traits.

XIII

When your aura is strong and resonates well with others, it is very easy for you to influence others. Be careful that you do not use this influencing ability in an unethical manner. Karma is real. When you act, you sow causes into the universe. When you sow causes into the universe, it is inevitable that you will reap their corresponding effects. A charismatic personality will help you rise to power, but whatever power you gain must be used wisely and compassionately. This is not to say you should not use the power and influence of your charismatic aura to increase your happiness in life. However, you must keep in mind the well-being of others and avoid inflicting suffering upon them by abusing your charismatic influence over them.

XIV

I would like to issue a warning. Do not think that how charismatic you are is the only factor that determines whether people like you. If you are mean to others, no one will like you, regardless of how charismatic you are. If you smell, no one will want to date you, regardless of how charismatic you are.

VXI

Let's consider a hypothetical person named John. When John was in middle school, he was very antisocial and shy. As a result, despite wanting a healthy social life, he was never able to establish one. Shortly before entering high school, his dad got a new job and his whole family had to move. He decided to reinvent himself into the kind of person with a healthy and active social life. He did his best to strike up conversations with others. He tried to act outgoing. He joined different clubs. However, at the end of a few weeks, he noticed something. No matter how friendly he tried to be towards others, or how outgoing he tried to act, people were just not inclined to be friends with him. He noticed that in some instances, people he had just met disliked him, even though he had done nothing wrong to them.

The problem was John's aura. It did not resonate well with others, so it repelled them. This is why John's efforts to attract others to himself and build up a circle of friends around himself failed.

VXI

Some actors are well-known and well-liked even though their acting ability is poor. Despite being bad actors, audiences love to see them perform. Their auras are strong and resonate well with the auras of those in the audience. There is an astra-mental attractive force between the actors and the audience members. This causes the audience members to like the actors.

Bonus Content: A Walk Down Memory Lane

Bonus Content: A Walk Down Memory Lane

The process of writing a book can be an emotional roller coaster. There are always so many decisions! Each book I've written has gone through many drafts. The first draft of *The Spirit of Magic* looked nothing like the final draft that was actually published. The same thing is true for both *The Elemental Equilibrium* and *The Covert Side of Initiation*, the book you are holding in your hands.

I can be a very verbose person, and that's often reflected in my writing. As a result, when it comes to finalizing the manuscripts for my books, much of the revision process centers on cutting out stuff that doesn't fit with the theme of the book. For example, in the first draft of *The Spirit of Magic*, there was a chapter about Druidry and a chapter about chaos magic. I ended up having to cut those out because they didn't fit with the theme of the book, which was the heart of magic (compassion, service, being a blessing to others, etc.). In addition, because the book was supposed to be about magic in general rather than the Bardon system specifically, I had to cut out many sections that were just about the Bardon system.

Cutting stuff out of manuscripts is always hard for me. It's necessary if I want my books to be organized, concise, and coherent, but it's hard because some of the stuff I cut out contains useful information—information I think people should know.

The Spirit of Magic was published in February of 2017. I'm currently writing these words on December 29th, 2017. It's been almost a year since my first book was published, and in that time, I've written two more books. In the process of revising my three books to get them ready for publication, I've had to cut out a lot of material. I thought it would be fun to end this first year of my career as a magical author by sharing all of the useful bits and pieces I've had to cut out of the early drafts of my books for one reason or another. We'll start with the bits and pieces I had to cut out of *The Spirit of Magic* and end with the bits and pieces I had to cut out of *The Covert Side of Initiation*, or rather, the main text of the book. I guess those bits and pieces still managed to end up in the final published version, but not in the way I originally anticipated.

Bits and Pieces Cut from *The Spirit of Magic*

The First Lesson

Anyone who intends to work through IIH should first internalize the following idea.

THERE ARE NO AUTHORITIES WHEN IT COMES TO THE BARDON SYSTEM.

Why do I insist that students of the Bardon system internalize this idea? There are several Bardonists who regularly write about the Bardon system. Some of them write about the Bardon system on their blogs. Others write about the Bardon system on their websites. Others write about the Bardon system in their books. These Bardonists are often viewed as experts on the Bardon system, and people usually believe whatever they write without question. I'm going to refer to these people as "prominent Bardonists" in this section. Rawn Clark and William Mistele are examples of prominent Bardonists.

So, to summarize what prominent Bardonists are and what they do, prominent Bardonists write about the Bardon system on their websites and blogs, as well as in their books. Their names are well-known amongst Bardonists, and they are greatly revered in the Bardon community. Prominent Bardonists are believed to have reached the advanced steps of IIH and to have extensive experience evoking the spirits of PME.

There is no magical force that prevents people from writing blogs or books about the Bardon system unless they have first worked through it. Therefore, even someone who is not past Step 1 could start a blog about the Bardon system or write a few books about the Bardon system. The information would come largely from speculation instead of from direct experience and would therefore be far less reliable than the direct-experience-based knowledge of someone who has truly worked through IIH. When you have reached the advanced steps of IIH, then when you read a blog post or book about the Bardon system, you can easily tell if the author is writing from direct experience and knows what he is talking about. However, most books about the Bardon system and blog posts about the Bardon system are targeted towards beginners. Beginners have a harder time discriminating between those writers who know what they are talking about and those who don't. When it comes to magical training in general, bad advice can set you back for years and even cause you to put yourself in danger. For that reason, I have written this section. When someone gives you advice, use your own intuition, common sense, and power of reason to analyze the advice. Do not think to yourself "Oh, this person is a well-known Bardonist blogger/author. He must be an authority on the Bardon system, and therefore I should just accept whatever advice he gives me."

Even in the case of someone who has truly worked through IIH, you should not indiscriminately accept whatever advice he gives you. Consider Rawn Clark and William Mistele. Both are prominent Bardonists who have truly worked through IIH and accumulated a great deal of practical experience with the work of PME and KTQ. However, even they should not be viewed as authorities. Despite their vast knowledge and deep understanding of the Bardon system, they occasionally make erroneous comments when discussing the Bardon system or writing about it.

Listen to Your Bodies

A long time ago, I was reading an occult book that contained instructions for an occult exercise. According to the book, practicing this exercise would make my astral body stronger. I began practicing this exercise each day. The exercise, however, actually made my astral body weaker. My astral body kept telling me that it was becoming weaker, but I didn't listen. I didn't notice the signals it was sending me, and the thought that the exercise was weakening my astral body never crossed my mind because the book clearly told me that this exercise would make my astral body stronger. Although the book's claim contradicted what my astral body was telling me, I foolishly chose to believe the book until I could no longer ignore the truth. It took me nearly two years to heal my astral body and bring it back to its prior level of strength. I had only been practicing the occult exercise for one month. Had I listened to my astral body earlier, I would have stopped practicing the exercise a lot sooner.

Now, at first, this might seem to have nothing to do with magical training in the Bardon system. After all, all of Bardon's exercises are safe if you have completed the prior exercises. Therefore, it seems like there is no need to listen to your bodies in case they alert you that you are doing something harmful to your mental, astral, or physical body.

However, what if you haven't truly completed all of the prior exercises in IIH before working on an exercise, but mistakenly thought you had? In that case, you might injure your bodies. If you don't pay attention to your bodies and listen to them, it might be a while before you notice, but during that time, you can do a lot of damage to them. Also, Bardon is not always the clearest writer. What if you misinterpret his instructions and do an exercise incorrectly? Performing a mental, astral, or physical exercise incorrectly can certainly harm your mental, astral, or physical body. In such an incident, you wouldn't realize at first that you are doing the exercise incorrectly, but if you listened to your bodies, you would realize quickly that something was wrong and reevaluate what you are doing.

Always listen to your bodies, whether it is your physical body, your astral body, or your mental body. Never ignore the messages they send you. If they tell you that you are doing something wrong, you are probably doing something wrong – even if you think you're doing everything right.

Building a Friendship with Your Mind

[Author's note: The following is an excerpt from my first book – *The Spirit of Magic: Rediscovering the Heart of our Sacred Art*. I include it because it is referenced in the next section.]

The first exercise of Step 1, thought-observation, is truly my favorite exercise in all of IIH. At first, you might think that the creation of the soul mirrors is my favorite exercise, after all, I am always talking about it and emphasizing its importance. I definitely believe creating the soul mirrors is the most important exercise in IIH, and one of the key things that separate Bardon's genuine magical system from the many occult systems in existence. Still, it's not my favorite exercise. Thought-observation is. I am a busy person, but sometimes, I'll go to a quiet place like the local library and practice thought observation for an hour, two hours, or even an entire afternoon. I don't do it because I want to advance along the magical path. I do it simply because I think it's fun.

You will be working with your mind a lot throughout your magical training. Have you ever worked with a coworker that you did not like and did not understand that well? It really sucks, doesn't it? Imagine if you could have worked with a friend you understood well instead. The experience would have been much more enjoyable, and you probably would have gotten much more done.

You should come to think of your mind as your friend. In order to build a friendship with your mind, you need to get to know it. That's what it's like the first few times you practice thought-observation. You are hanging out with your mind so you can get to know it better in order to become friends with it. Later on, when you continue to practice thought-observation even when you are in the advanced stages of training, you are hanging out with your friend because, well, that's what friends do.

The Step 1 Mental Exercises

There are four exercises in this section.

1. The first is to observe your thoughts.
2. The second is to center your awareness on what you are presently doing.

3. The third is to hold just one thought in your mind.
4. The fourth is to empty your mind of all thoughts.

I want to begin this section by introducing an analogy. Think of a room filled with cats. The room is your mind. Each cat is a thought. The first mental exercise is about watching the cats. When you can do this easily for ten minutes without becoming distracted or absent-minded, you can move on to the next exercise. The fourth exercise is about emptying the room of all cats.

Emptying the room of all cats should be a relatively easy task for someone who can see, but it is nearly impossible for someone who is blind. If you're blind, you could be standing in the middle of a room filled with cats thinking it is empty. In reality, the room is filled with cats, but you aren't aware of them because you're blind and can't see them. A lot of people start off blind. They sit down to do this first exercise, try to observe their thoughts, and then think that they have no thoughts. They either try to create thoughts to observe or simply move on to the next exercise. Both courses of action are serious errors, and they arise from a lack of understanding of what is going on. It isn't that you have no thoughts. It's that there are many thoughts running through your mind, but you just haven't learned to be aware of them. Thus, people who sit down to do the thought-observation exercise and think they have no thoughts to observe are like blind people in a room full of cats thinking it is empty.

There are two stages of mastery of the first mental exercise.

1. Get the hang of observing your thoughts.
2. Observe your thoughts for ten minutes.

The first stage of mastery is about learning to see. Thus, when you've completed this stage, you've gone from being a blind person to a person who can see. The second stage is about actually watching the cats. You start by watching the cats for five minutes each day until you can do this easily. Then, you extend the amount of time you watch the cats by one minute each day until you can easily watch the cats for ten minutes. When you can watch the cats for ten minutes without trouble, you have completed this exercise and can move on to the next one.

The second stage of mastery is pretty straightforward. It's just a matter of practicing observing your thoughts each day. The first stage of mastery, getting the hang of observing your thoughts, is a lot trickier. This is where most students struggle. One thing that makes this part of the process especially confusing is that Bardon tells you to "observe" your thoughts. Human language is not perfect, and sometimes you have to do the best you can do. "Observe" is not a bad word to use, however, unfortunately, it gives the impression that the thoughts passing through your mind appear as visual images. This is not true. The fact of the matter is, there is no good way to describe what a thought "looks" like when you "observe" it as it passes through your mind.

Instead of "observe," I prefer to say "be aware of." Thus, while most Bardonists refer to the first mental exercises as "thought-observation," I usually call it "thought-awareness" in my own notes.

So, how do you get the hang of being aware of your thoughts? Sit down in in a chair and just be aware. Don't try to be aware of your thoughts. Don't try to be aware of your breath. Don't try to be aware of your bodily sensations. Just be aware.[27] Don't do this for too long. Spend a few minutes at most once or twice a day doing this. As you practice being aware, your awareness will sharpen. Slowly, over the days/weeks you practice being aware, the sensitivity of your awareness will grow so that you are aware of subtle things (like mental activities) you previously weren't aware of. The scope of your awareness will expand to encompass things it previously did not encompass, like all the thoughts running through your mind that you previously did not notice. At this point, you have gotten the hang of being aware of (AKA "observing") your thoughts, and therefore have completed the first stage of mastery for this exercise. Now it's just a matter of practicing remaining aware of your thoughts until you can do so attentively for ten minutes without becoming distracted, absent-minded, or falling into a daydream.

The second mental exercise was discussed in great detail in Chapter 4.

The third mental exercise consists of holding a single thought in your mind. I suggest getting a pencil and piece of paper and making a list of thoughts to hold in your mind. A list of potential thoughts to consider is as follows:

All nations are at peace with each other.

I am successful

The economy is healthy.

I am healthy.

My guardian angel loves me.

It is inevitable I will become an adept.

I am responsible.

This exercise involves holding a well-formulated thought in your mind. It is a well-known magical principle that when a strong mind formulates a thought, that thought has a tendency to manifest as reality. For this reason, I choose to use relatively positive thoughts for this exercise. If I were to focus on a thought like "I suck," then that thought might manifest as reality, and that would clearly not be good for me. You might be asking yourself if focusing on the thought "I am successful" will manifest success in your life. It might, but please be aware that this isn't the point of the exercise. The idea behind using positive thoughts for this exercise isn't to manifest positivity in your life, but to avoid accidentally manifesting negativity in your life. Neutral thoughts such as "My cat likes milk" could also be used, but positive thoughts are usually more enjoyable to work with. If, by focusing on a thought like "I am successful," you do end up manifesting success in your life, then that should just be seen as a bonus.[28]

The final mental exercise in Step 1 is to empty your mind of all thoughts. This exercise is often referred to by Bardonists as "VOM," which stands for "vacancy of mind." A ton of Bardonists have trouble with this exercise. Look around on any online Bardon group or forum and you'll be sure to find many people struggling with this exercise and asking for tips or advice. This always cracks me up. VOM is by far the easiest exercise in IIH, but this is only the case if you are truly proficient in thought-observation.

Imagine that a bull has escaped from a pen and it's your job to return the bull back again. Imagine that you have to wrestle the with to bull to achieve this. This is a very difficult and exhausting task. You might even strain yourself and get hurt. Since bulls are much stronger than humans, you're probably not going to succeed. You will end up being very frustrated though.

Now imagine that you and the bull are very good friends. You have a great relationship with each other. You're both familiar with each other and comfortable with each other. In this case, it would be very easy to lead the bull back into the pen. In fact, it would take almost no effort at all.

If you've read Appendix A, then you can probably see where I'm going with this analogy. It is difficult for most people to wrestle their minds into a state of emptiness and stillness. If you're good friends with your mind, however, then it should be very easy to lead your mind into a state of emptiness and stillness. Thus, if you invest in the thought-observation exercise, you'll get a big return when you practice VOM. Instead of wrestling an angry bull back into a pen, you'll find yourself gently leading a friendly bull back.

Note that there are some cheap tricks you can use to get the bull back into the pen. You can put food in the pen to entice it. You can shoot it with a tranquilizer dart so that it becomes unconscious and then carry it into the pen. There are all sorts of these cheap tricks you can try. Similarly, there are all sorts of cheap tricks you can do to get your mind into a state of emptiness. They're floating everywhere around the Bardon community. Just go onto an online Bardon forum and make a post asking for help with VOM. You'll find that tons of people will reply with cheap tricks to empty your mind of thoughts. There are two reasons you should ignore these tricks. First, they're kind of cheating, and thus, relying on them to complete this exercise is a course of action that will come back to bite you in the butt later. Secondly, you shouldn't need them. The man who is good friends with a bull and can lead it gently back into the pen doesn't need to rely on bait or tranquilizer darts to help him. Similarly, if you're truly proficient in thought-observation and have gained a good familiarity and comfort with your mind, it should be very easy for your lead your mind into a state of emptiness and stillness without the use of tricks.

Tricks

Tricks don't really have a place in magic. In other disciplines and situations, tricks may be appropriate. For example, when traveling by airplane, most suitcases look very similar to each other. If someone asks you if you want to know a trick that will help you identify your suitcase quickly, you should say yes. There is a trick for that, by the way. Tie a piece of bright string to the handle of your suitcase. If you see a suitcase with the string tied to the handle, you'll immediately know it's yours and won't have to examine it carefully.

If someone asks you if you want to know a trick that will quickly empty your mind, you should say no. When it comes to attaining VOM, you should be able to do it without tricks. Now, there's a difference between giving someone advice and teaching someone a "trick." There's nothing wrong with giving advice. As for all of the "tricks" I've seen with regards to magical training, most of them are just ways to trick you into thinking you've mastered a particular exercise when you've come nowhere close.

Let's say you want to win a swordfight. There are a number of cheap tricks you could use. You can carry dirt in your pocket and throw it into your opponent's eyes. You can slip poison into his food before the fight. You can use a gun disguised as a sword instead of an actual sword during the fight. These cheap tricks will allow you to win the swordfight, but they don't mean you are proficient in sword fighting. If your real goal was to win the fight, you've succeeded. If your real goal was to demonstrate your proficiency in sword fighting, you've failed, even though you've won the fight. Similarly, your real goal isn't to empty your mind.

It's to become proficient in a certain method of emptying your mind. Thus, using cheap tricks to empty your mind doesn't mean you are proficient in the fourth mental exercise.

The Cicada and the Wren

There is a Taoist story of a cicada and a wren. Someone told the cicada and wren that there are birds that can fly thousands of miles. The cicada and the wren discussed this claim and decided that it was bullshit. The cicada said to the wren "We both know that the furthest anyone can fly is that tree over there, and even that takes an enormous amount of effort."

Some people claim that working through Bardon's system is impossible because it is too difficult and takes too much effort. Other people claim that the methods and manner of evocation Bardon describes in PME are impossible to carry out because they require a level of magical ability that, realistically speaking, no human magician can achieve. When people make this claim, I always think of the story of the cicada and the wren.

When the cicada and the wren announced that it was impossible for birds to fly thousands of miles just because they themselves could barely fly to a nearby tree, they revealed a lot about themselves. For one thing, they revealed their own low standards when it comes to the art of flying. In addition, they revealed their willingness to completely ignore enormous piles of evidence sitting right in front of them. After all, anyone can look up at the sky and see birds flying vast distances.

Similarly, people who claim that Bardon's system is impossible or that his evocation methods require unrealistically high levels of magical skill reveal the same things about themselves. Bardon's system is not impossibly difficult; in fact, it is as easy as a valid system of magical training can possibly be. The magical skills taught in IIH and their accompanying standards of mastery are the bare minimum required to become a genuine magician. As for the impossibility of working through IIH or using the techniques of PME, Rawn and Bill both have websites where they discuss their journey through IIH and their own experiences using the techniques of PME to contact the elemental sovereigns and the ruling spirits of the planetary spheres.

Through dedication and hard work, any cicada or wren can transform himself into a falcon capable of flying thousands of miles. However, in order to do this, the cicada or wren must first be willing to believe that it is in fact possible to fly thousands of miles.

<u>Friendship</u>

Magical training involves building many friendships, including friendships with the following:

1. Your mental body/mind
2. Your astral body/emotions
3. Your physical body
4. Initiation into Hermetics
5. Saturn

I've already discussed building a friendship with your mind in the previously quoted passage from *The Spirit of Magic*.

For the same reasons you should build a friendship with your mental body, you should build a friendship with your astral body and physical body. Just as building a friendship with your mental body begins with getting to know it (via thought-observation), building friendships with your astral and physical body begins with getting to know them as well. Getting to know your astral body begins with creating the soul mirrors. Getting to know your physical body can be a complex process, and the best way to approach this process differs on a case by case basis. Bill has written an excellent article detailing one possible approach to this process.[29]

Building a friendship with IIH also begins with getting to know it. IIH contains a system of magical training. Many times, people read IIH because their preconceived notions about magical training systems distort their interpretation of the text. When you read IIH for the first time, it's best to forget everything you know or think you know about magical training and let the book speak for yourself. Only someone who can do this can truly understand IIH, and only someone who truly understands IIH can become friends with the book. It may even be a good idea to read through the book cover to cover once a year to really familiarize yourself with its contents.

Saturn's goal is to help you become more mature. Helping someone is a great way to become friends with him. To become friends with Saturn, help him help you become more mature. The best way to do this is to introspect regularly and persistently use the six-pronged attack to transform yourself for the better.

A Note on Bill's Commentary on Thought-Observation

In Bill's commentary on thought-observation, he writes a lot about remembering your thoughts while observing them. This isn't actually a part of the exercise. It comes from a misinterpretation of an awkward translation of IIH. For more information, see the following link:

http://www.abardoncompanion.de/Remember.html

Chakras

A lot of Bardonists are interested in yoga, and therefore interested in chakras and kundalini. Of course, there is nothing wrong with being interested in these subjects or reading about them, but experimenting with these subjects can be dangerous. For more information, read the following two links:

http://www.abardoncompanion.de/Chakras.html

http://www.abardoncompanion.de/Kundalini.html

The Mistake of Intentionally Creating Thoughts During Thought-Observation

When many people practice the first mental exercise of Step 1 for the first time, they sit down to observe their thoughts only to find that they have no thoughts. Now, as I've pointed out repeatedly in my past writings, they do have thoughts; they just haven't learned to be aware of them yet. In any case, one mistake they often make is that they try creating thoughts to observe. Now, if this mental exercise is about observing/being aware of your thoughts, then it makes sense to do this. It's still a mistake, but at least it's a mistake that makes sense. The thing is, this exercise isn't about observing/being aware of your thoughts. It's about observing/being aware of your mind. Thus, "mind-observation" or "mind-awareness" would be a better name for this exercise, rather than "thought-observation."

Many Bardonists think of the mind as a jar. Let's say that a thought is represented by a marble. The first mental exercise of Step 1 is about looking into the jar. It doesn't matter if the jar is empty or filled with marbles. Since the exercise is about looking into the jar, rather than looking at marbles in the jar, there's no need to put marbles in the jar if it seems empty to you. This jar/marble model is why Bardonists often use the phrase "empty your mind."

Yogis think of the mind as an object made of something called "chitta." Thoughts are waves ("vritti") on this chitta. Think of your mind as an ocean, and each thought as a wave on the ocean. The first mental exercise is about observing the ocean. It doesn't matter if there are any waves on the ocean, since the exercise is about observing/being aware of the ocean, not waves on the ocean. Thus, there is no need to create waves to observe. This object/wave model is why yogis often use the phrase "still your mind."

In any case, from what I've written so far, it should be clear why trying to create thoughts to observe is a mistake. If you try to do this, you've missed the point of the exercise. Just sit down and observe/be aware of your mind and what is going on in it. If it is empty/still, then that's fine. If it's filled/busy, that's fine too.

What is it like to observe/be aware of your thoughts?

Many people ask me what it's like to observe your thoughts. I think a quote by Lao Tzu sums it up perfectly—"Those who know don't say; those who say don't know." In other words, those who try to explain to you what it is like to observe your thoughts don't know what it is like to observe your thoughts. Those who do know what it is like to observe your thoughts won't try to explain what it is like to observe your thoughts. They'll know that due to the inadequacies of human language, there is just no good way to explain/describe what it is like.[30] You'll just have to experience the process for yourself.

Use of Will

In the first edition text of *A Bardon Companion*, Rawn writes the following.

> *"The third type of meditation is titled "Mastery of Thoughts" and involves the attainment of a vacancy of mind or an absence of thoughts. For those unfamiliar with meditation, this is often the most difficult task. It requires a good deal of will power and persistent effort. When thoughts intrude, you must learn to willfully shun them and regain your emptiness. I assure you that this is not an impossible task."*

I have a lot of problems with this description/explanation of the fourth mental exercise in Step 1. This exercise shouldn't require a lot of willpower. If a bull doesn't like you, then yes you will need a lot of strength to wrestle it into a pen. If you are friends with a bull, you shouldn't need any strength at all to gently guide it back into the pen. Similarly, if you have become good friends with your mind after practicing the first exercise for a while, it shouldn't take a lot of willpower to gently guide it into a state of emptiness and stillness. If the VOM exercise seems impossible to you the first time you do it, you don't need to be reassured that the exercise isn't impossible. You need to be told to go back to the first exercise and deepen your proficiency in it.

The Magic of Water

In the first edition of *A Bardon Companion*, Rawn explains the conscious breathing exercises and then writes the following.

> *"The next two sections are titled 'The Conscious Intake of Nourishment' and 'The Magic of Water.' These techniques are based upon the same principles as the mystery of breath—an idea is attached by the mind to the akasha principle of the physical substance."*

This is not true. Conscious eating and conscious breathing rely on the magic of akasha. The techniques taught in the magic of water section rely on—you guessed it—the magic of water. More accurately, they rely on the properties of the root of the water element—the magnetic fluid. As I pointed out repeatedly in my second book, akasha and the magnetic fluid are not the same.

In the second edition of *A Bardon Companion*, Rawn makes the same mistake again. He begins his second edition commentary on the Step 1 physical exercises with some comments on the stretching exercise and then proceeds to write the following:

> *"The next sections on the 'mystery of breathing,' the 'conscious reception of food,' and the 'magic of water' are all rooted in a single, very simplistic principle and technique. The principle behind them is the fact that the akasha, which is a natural part of all substance, attracts and captures thoughts and ideas, especially intentionally projected thoughts and ideas. So the*

technique simply takes advantage of this natural process by turning it into an intentional, conscious act."

While Rawn's comments are true for conscious breathing and conscious eating, they are incorrect when it comes to techniques using the magic of water. The properties of akasha do not play a role in the mechanics of these techniques.

<u>The Seven Years Myth</u>

In the first edition of *A Bardon Companion*, Rawn gives the following response to a question asking whether the student needs to impregnate every meal or drink he consumes.

"No, you don't have to, but by doing it every chance you get, you will be increasing the effectiveness of this technique. Eventually, it will become second nature to you and no one else will even notice that you are doing it. If I remember correctly, it takes about seven years for your body to completely renew every cell. You can, in theory, insert your thought into the structure of each new cell that is born and thus, directly transform your physical body."

It is not true that your body renews all its cells every seven years. This used to be a popular myth but was debunked. In any case, how long it takes your physical body to renew its physical cells doesn't matter too much. The focus of the work of self-transformation is the transformation of the astra-mental body, not the physical body. Your physical body will definitely change, in this way cementing the personality transformations you initiate within yourself through the techniques of conscious eating and conscious breathing, but the direct and intended impact of these techniques is on the astra-mental body.

Solving Problems

Some people think working through IIH involves nothing more than following the instructions in the practice section the same way you'd follow the instructions on a can of soup to make soup. Yes, a large part of training in the Bardon system does consist of just following the instructions in IIH, but that doesn't mean you won't encounter problems or obstacles as you work through IIH. Here are nine methods you can use to solve the problems you encounter along your path.

1. Adapt
2. Transform
3. Research
4. Ask
5. Pray
6. Dissect
7. Practice outside exercises
8. Use ingenuity
9. Take a break

The first method is to adapt. Let's say you are struggling with the visual plastic imagination exercise. After a few weeks, you are no better at this exercise than before. You could try working on the auditory plastic imagination exercise instead. In his commentary, Rawn relates a story about a guy who hadn't made any progress with the visual plastic imagination exercise even after a year of practice. He then switched to working with the auditory plastic imagination and quickly became proficient in it. Becoming proficient in the auditory plastic imagination helped develop the part of his mind pertaining to the plastic imagination in general. Therefore, when he tried the visual plastic imagination exercises again, he was successful.

The second method is to transform. Let's say that you are having trouble with the conscious eating exercise because you keep getting frustrated while trying to impregnate the food and, as a result, end up impregnating the food with your frustration instead of whatever positive quality you originally wanted to impregnate it with. If you transform yourself into a patient person, then you won't get frustrated, and therefore, you won't have this problem. If you are struggling to find time to practice your magical exercises, you can transform yourself into a more efficient person. This will help free up time that you can use to practice your magical exercises. If you encounter a problem in your training, check to see if transforming yourself by developing a certain positive trait or eliminating a certain negative trait will solve the problem or help solve the problem.

The third method is to research. Let's say you are having trouble with the conscious breathing exercise. You could read the section about conscious breathing in Rawn's commentary, which contains a lot of great tips. This is an example of doing research. Or, let's say you are having trouble developing the trait of being organized. There are many great websites about staying organized. A simple Google search will lead you to many. Looking through them is another example of doing research.

The fourth method is to ask. You could email someone like William Mistele describing your problem and asking for advice. You could join an online Bardon-themed group, describe your problem to its members, and ask for advice. You could ask practitioners of other spiritual traditions that practice the same exercises as the Bardon system for advice. For example, VOM is practiced by some Buddhist traditions, so you could talk to experienced Buddhist meditators and ask for their advice.

The fifth method is to pray to God for help in finding a solution and solving the problem. Do not underestimate the power of prayer. According to the adept Stylianos Atteshlis, no prayer ever goes unanswered. When I read this many years ago, I took his statement on faith because I realized he was a genuine adept and therefore trusted him and his teachings. I prayed regularly throughout my training. Later on, when my magical skills developed and I saw and understood the mechanics behind prayer, I realized that his statement is correct and no longer had to take it on faith.

The sixth method is to analyze the problem and dissect it into many smaller problems. Once you've done this, you can tackle the smaller problems one by one. For example, if you are struggling to find out what element a trait on your black soul mirror belongs to, break the trait up into smaller traits and figure out what element each smaller trait belongs to.

The seventh method is to practice exercises from outside the Bardon system that you believe will help supplement your work with Bardon's system. For example, in the last section of the next chapter, I give an exercise to help you become continually present-minded. The exercise I give is one I created and is not a part of the Bardon system, but if you are having trouble with the Bardon system's present-mindedness exercise, you can practice the exercise I give.

The eighth method is to use your ingenuity to come up with a solution. When I was working through Step 2, I messed up my etheric body after practicing pore breathing incorrectly. To repair my etheric body, I had to invent my own brand new system of qigong. This involved creating and practicing qigong exercises that were specifically designed to mend the etheric injuries I had inflicted upon myself. This is kind of an extreme example, but it's an example nonetheless.

The ninth method is to take a break from trying to solve the problem. This could involve temporarily suspending your training (or a part of your training) and resuming it after some time has passed. You might find that for some reason the problem has either disappeared or become much easier to solve. For example, visualization used to be very difficult for me, so at first I really struggled with the visual plastic imagination exercises of Step 2. I kind of gave them up for a week because they were frustrating, exhausting, and strained my mind. When I resumed practicing the visualization exercises after a one week break, they were easy. I have no idea why. Sometimes you just need a break.

When it comes to using these methods, there are two important things to remember. The first is that these methods don't cover all possible methods of solving a problem. The second is that some problems are caused by karma. If you don't deal with the karmic root of a problem, then either the problem won't go away no matter what you do, or another problem will pop up to take its place once you get rid of it. Dealing with the karmic root of a problem usually involves becoming more mature in some specific way. If you have reason to believe that a problem you are dealing with has a karmic root, then introspection and contemplation is the best way to identify what you need to do to deal with the karmic root.

A Comment on Pore Breathing

There are four exercises in the physical section of Step 2. Bardon describes the exercise of pore breathing first, but I highly recommend you wait until you have mastered your asana before beginning this exercise. I make this suggestion for three reasons.

The first reason is that doing this exercise in a mastered asana will make it easier for you. You'll be comfortable with your body, and therefore, your body won't distract you. Thus, you can focus all of your attention on the tactile plastic imagination, which is used to create the sensation of the vital force flowing in and out of your body through your pores.

The second reason is that by the time you master your asana, there's a good chance you will already have some experience with the tactile plastic imagination, which is used in this exercise. Remember that plastic imagination training constitutes the mental part of this step's work. With pore breathing, you begin by imagining the sensation of the vital force passing through your skin into and out of your body. With practice, this imagined sensation becomes much more than just an imagined sensation, as the vital force really will be moving in and out of you via your skin. If you already have some experience with the tactile plastic imagination from the Step 2 mental training, this will make it much easier to begin this exercise.

The third reason is that pore breathing will greatly increase the amount of your amount of magical power. Through this technique, Bardonists accumulate enormous amounts of energy within themselves, allowing them to accomplish magical feats that many modern occultists would consider impossible fantasies. As a result, when you practice pore breathing, you are reaching for a lot of magical power. Divine Providence, through the influence of the Saturn principle, restricts the amount of magical power individuals have according to the level of their maturity. If an immature person reaches for magical power, the Saturn principle will really crack down hard on him. If a mature person reaches for magical power, Saturn won't crack down on him. The universe is fine with him having magical power because he is mature and therefore able to use that power responsibly. By the time you have mastered your asana, you will have spent quite a bit of time on the self-transformation work described in the astral section of this step. This self-transformation work will greatly increase your maturity, putting you in a better position to reach for magical power.

The Clairvoyance of a Magician

In IIH, Bardon uses the phrase "clairvoyance of a magician" in order to contrast the clairvoyance of a magician from other types of clairvoyance. I've always thought this was interesting. Many students of magic think that clairvoyance is clairvoyance, but as Bardon points out, this is not the case. There are different types of clairvoyance. The student of magic should not focus on developing clairvoyance, but on developing the clairvoyance of a magician.

The clairvoyance of a magician is developed naturally over a period of time. It is not developed suddenly and forcefully through the use of drugs or intense ascetic or concentration practices. Furthermore, the clairvoyance of a magician is developed directly. In some systems of magical training, students develop clairvoyance indirectly by practicing exercises that require the use of clairvoyance, such as scrying. This is a bit like someone trying to learn arithmetic by taking a calculus class. Calculus uses some arithmetic, so by taking a calculus class, you can learn some arithmetic along the way, but it is better to learn arithmetic directly by taking an arithmetic class. Similarly, it is better to learn clairvoyance first before attempting something that uses clairvoyance like scrying, rather than learning clairvoyance by attempting to scry.

The clairvoyance of a magician is directly proportional to the purity of his soul. For this reason, the magician should always strive to improve himself and become an ever nobler and more righteous and compassionate person.

The clairvoyance of a magician is fully under the will of the magician. In other words, he has complete control over it, and is able to turn his clairvoyance on and off whenever he wants to. Some people are clairvoyant but cannot turn off their clairvoyance. Thus, they are always confused because they are never sure whether something they see is physical or exists purely in the inner planes. Often, these people end up in mental hospitals. Their clairvoyance is not the clairvoyance of a magician.

The Dangers of Flawed and Poorly Constructed Exercises

There are many magical exercises that are inherently dangerous because they are poorly constructed and flawed. Despite the fact that they are widely practiced, few people experience or suffer from the dangers that can arise from these exercises. This is because the typical person practicing these exercises is protected by his weak will, inability to concentrate, and poor imagination. Once you strengthen your will, learn to concentrate, and develop your imagination, then you have the potential to inflict great harm onto yourself with your will, concentration, and imagination. For this reason, for most of my magical training, I have more or less stuck solely to the exercises of IIH because I know that, when practiced correctly, they pose no danger to those who are ready to practice them.

Common Mistakes

The following is a list of the most common mistakes people make when attempting to work through IIH.

- Sitting down to practice thought-observation, thinking you have no thoughts, and then trying to create thoughts or move on to the next mental exercise.

- Putting more effort into the creation of the black soul mirror than into the creation of the white soul mirror.

- Skipping the exercise that consists of stretching in the morning. Contrary to what some have claimed, this exercise isn't just about physical health. The more flexible a balloon is, the more air it can hold before it pops. Similarly, the more flexible your body is, the more etheric energy it can hold before it becomes strained. Thus, before you begin accumulating the vital force in Step 3, it is imperative that you have a flexible body.

- Trying to fill their food or air with "energy" when practicing conscious eating or conscious breathing.

- Working with two dimensional shapes instead of simple three dimensional objects when practicing visualization in Step 2. Bardon says you practice visualizing simple small objects like buttons, chess pieces, paperclips, and bottle caps. A lot of people try to visualize simple two dimensional shapes like a red triangle, or a green square, or an orange circle, thinking that this will be easier because they only have to worry about two dimensions and one color, instead of three dimensions and several colors. In reality, the opposite is true. The extra dimension and the details of the object give you more to grab onto, which makes it easier to hold the image in your mind and to hold it still.

Common Misconceptions

In this section, I wish to address some common misconceptions Bardonists have.

Inspiration

- The Bardon system is not yoga. The purpose of the Bardon system is not to liberate its students from the wheel of samsara, but to teach them how to embody the highest forms of wisdom and power in order to make the world a more joyful and wonderful place to live in. Enlightenment and liberation are important milestones along the magical path, but are not the end goal.

Theory

- No, you do not have to memorize the information about the electric and magnetic parts of the body in the diet section of the theory part of IIH.

- The etheric body and the astral matrix are not the same thing. Bardon explains the difference between them several times in IIH and PME. The etheric body consists of the vital force in the body and the channels through which the vital force flows. The astral matrix is a construct made from the electric and magnetic fluids that facilitates the transfer of information and energy between the physical and astral bodies.

Practice

- You should not strive to have an equal number of traits on your black and white soul mirrors. You should, however, strive to have at least 100 items on each mirror.

- The end goal of the soul mirror creation process is not just to have lists of your positive and negative traits. Another end goal of the soul mirror creation process is to learn how to introspect. This is why you must analyze yourself. You cannot rely on others to analyze you for you.

- Conscious breathing is not pranayama.

- When Bardon says to start with seven breaths while practicing conscious breathing, he doesn't mean to inhale but divide the inhalation into seven segments. He means to inhale fully seven times with each inhalation followed by a full exhalation.

- Using the magic of water does not consist of impregnating water with a positive quality and drinking it. It consists of washing your hands or showering in cold water and willing the magnetic fluid in the water to absorb your negative character traits and carry them down the drain.

- In the Step 2 plastic imagination exercises, the sensations you create should seem just as real as if they came from a physical source. For example, let's say you place a paper clip in front of you and then visualize another paper clip next to it. You should have a hard time determining which paper clip is the real one and which is the visualized one. If anyone tells you to content yourself with lower standards than this, don't listen.

- The purpose of the Step 2 asana practice is not to develop willpower. Its purpose is to provide you with a posture you can remain in comfortably. This allows you to focus on your magical exercises without being distracted by bodily discomforts.

- It doesn't matter what the beads on your Bardonian mala are made of. The sole purpose of the Bardonian mala is to do your counting for you. You use it to count distractions while meditating, to count the number of breaths you've taken while pore breathing the elements, and the number of times you've repeated an affirmation while practicing autosuggestion. At no point in the work of IIH are you accumulating energy into the beads, contrary to what some people have claimed, so they don't have to be made out of crystals or some special substance.

- The astral exercises of Step 7 are not meant to develop your astral senses from scratch. As a result of your work in the previous steps, you astral senses will already have been partially opened, and may even be fully open. The Step 7 astral exercises are just meant to finish the process of opening your astral senses, not start it.

Bits and Pieces Cut from *The Elemental Equilibrium*

<u>A Lesson from Bialode</u>

In Bill's essay on the Earthzone spirit Bialode, he tries to explain what it is like to exist and interact with the universe the way this spirit does.

"You can hold something within your mind so every aspect of its energy and every facet of its being are contained within your awareness; you can enter into it and transform it; you can shape or recreate anything that exists beginning either from its core or by exerting an external influence."

When it comes to the work of self-transformation, you take responsibility for your personality. In order to do this, you work with your personality traits. You enter into your personality traits and transform them. You shape and recreate them. You can transform a personality trait from the inside out (conscious eating, conscious breathing, and autosuggestion), or from the outside in (volition). Some people view self-transformation as a process of eliminating your negative traits and developing their opposite positive traits. This is a valid way of thinking about the process. Other people view self-transformation as a process of transmuting your negative traits into their opposite positive traits. This is a different but equally valid way of thinking about the process.

As the passage from Bill's Bialode essay shows, if you want to fully transform a negative trait, you need to "hold it within your mind so every aspect of its energy and every facet of its being are contained within your awareness." In other words, you must thoroughly understand the trait, every aspect of the trait, and every facet of the trait's essence. Making your soul mirrors isn't enough to get you to that level. Let's say you possess the trait of impatience and put this trait on your black soul mirror. Your black soul mirror can now tell you that you possess the trait of impatience, but that's all it can tell you. You need to know a lot more about impatience than just the fact that you possess it. In fact, you don't just need to know about impatience. You need to know about YOUR impatience, after all, every personality that possesses this trait expresses it in its own unique manner.

We all know that introspection is an important part of the magical path. When you introspect, you do so with the intent of understand yourself or a part of yourself. When you introspect while making the soul mirrors, for example, you do so with the intent of understanding your personality. Once you've made your soul mirrors and begun the process of self-transformation, you need to do more introspection, but this time with the intent of understanding the specific negative trait you are working to eliminate/transmute. In the case of daydreaming at inappropriate times, you might reflect back upon your life and ask yourself the following questions.

1. What are some instances in the past where I have daydreamed at inappropriate times?
2. What are some of the biggest negative consequences I have had to face because of I daydreamed at inappropriate times?
3. What are some consequences I may face in the future if I continue to daydream at inappropriate times?
4. What is the purpose behind my negative trait of daydreaming at inappropriate times?
5. What are some less self-destructive ways I could fulfill this purpose?

A possible set of answers to these questions is as follows.

1. In the past, I would often daydream during lectures instead of paying attention to what the professor was saying.

2. Because I didn't learn anything in the lectures because I was daydreaming instead of paying attention, I didn't know how to do the homework and did poorly on exams.

3. In the future, I will continue do poorly on exams, suffer academically and may graduate with a low GPA.

4. I live a boring life but desire to live an interesting life. I daydream about doing exciting and interesting things as a way of satisfying my desire to live an interesting life.

5. I could develop a healthy social life, engage in various extracurricular activities, and study abroad.

It's by asking questions like this and gaining a better understanding of your impatience that you eventually gain the ability to "hold your impatience within your mind so every aspect of its energy and every facet of its being are contained within your awareness." This gives you a kind of power over the trait that reflects omnipotence. Bill writes that "this power generates a confidence that you can get done whatever you need to do." In this case, what you need to do is transmute the negative trait into its opposite positive trait, and when you understand the negative trait to this degree, you will indeed be confident in your ability to do that.

<u>The True Name of a Negative Trait</u>

Bill writes the following in his essay on Aphtiph.

"There was once a magical theory which stated that if you knew something's magical name, you had power over that thing. This wasn't an external way of knowing. To know another's magical name meant that you were one with its sources of inspiration. You embodied the energies and elements which made it

what it is—you are everything which grants it life, health, beauty, and wholeness."

At some point or another, we've all come across the idea that knowing the "true name" of someone or something grants you complete power over that person or that thing. This magical idea is found in Egyptian mythology, the Earthsea cycle, the Inheritance series, and numerous other forms of magical lore. In modern fiction, when this idea is present, the "true name" of someone or something is usually a literal name—a series of letters to be pronounced in a certain way. For example, in *A Wizard of Earthsea* there is a dragon whose true name is Yevaud. Geb knows this dragon's true name is Yevaud and therefore has control over the dragon. He can use this true name to get the dragon to do his bidding. The reality of the matter is that knowing something's true name is a metaphor for having a deep, full, and comprehensive understanding that thing. This understanding is so great that it allows you to perceive the world the way the thing does and comprehend its essence as easily if you yourself embodied that same essence. This full understanding gives you full power over that thing.

If you want to eliminate a negative trait or transmute it into its opposite positive trait, you need power over that trait. It is best to know the negative trait's true name because then you can get it to do whatever you want it to do—diminish, cease to exist, transform, transmute, etc. To learn a negative trait's true name, you need to understand it at all levels, from the level of physical action to the level of the inspiration/purpose that was the reason for that negative trait's formation.

<u>Incident Analysis</u>

Incident analysis is a technique used by Bardonists to come to a better understanding of one of their traits. This technique involves examining and reflecting upon a specific incident in which the trait influenced your actions. To use this technique, start by asking yourself the following questions.

1. What happened before the incident?
2. What happened during the incident?
3. What happened after the incident?
4. What should I have done different before the incident?
5. What should I have done differently during the incident?
6. What should I have done differently after the incident?

For example, let's say you are working to eliminate irritability from your personality and wish to use incident analysis to better understand your irritability. Start by picking an incident where irritability influenced your actions. Then, begin analyzing this incident by asking yourself the six questions listed above.

For example, let's say the incident you chose was a heated argument you had with your wife.

Question 1: Before the incident, I was at work. I had a bad day at work because some ideas I proposed during a meeting were ridiculed. This put me in a bad mood that remained with me through the rest of the day and while driving home. When I walked through the front door of your house, I was still in a bad mood.

Question 2: My wife asked me how my day was. I snapped at her not to ask me these kinds of questions. She became upset because I snapped at her and told me she was just trying to be friendly. She reprimanded me for snapping at her. Despite the fact that I did snap at her, I denied snapping at her and told her she was overly sensitive and that this is why she thought I snapped at her when I didn't. We then spent some time arguing about whether or not I had snapped at her.

Question 3: I went to my study and sat in a chair reading until dinnertime.

Question 4: I should not have proposed those ideas at the meeting. They were in fact ridiculous. I just wanted to say something, but didn't realize that I shouldn't say anything if I have nothing useful or insightful to say. Also, when I realized I was in a bad mood, I should have used the magical exhalation should expel the bad mood out of myself. I also could have used magical washing to wash it down the drain.

Question 5: I should not have snapped at my wife. Having snapped at my wife, I should have apologized to her instead of denying it.

Question 6: Instead of going to my room, I should have apologized to her.

These six questions will help you begin the process of analyzing an incident, but there are still many more questions you can ask yourself after working thought these six. Examples of other questions you can ask yourself include the following:

Are there any similarities between this incident and other incidents that involved the same trait?

> What can I do to prevent similar incidents from happening again?
>
> What did this incident teach me about my irritability?
>
> What can I do to repair the damage I created during this incident?
>
> What could I have done before the incident to make it worse?
>
> What could I have done during the incident to make it worse?
>
> What could I have done after the incident to make it worse?

Ambition

My friend Greg and I were once talking about another friend named Anna. During our conversation, Greg said something along the lines of "Anna's greatest strength—her ambition—is also her greatest weakness." This statement was true. Anna's ambition drove her to achieve some of her greatest successes. However, it had also brought her into danger and almost destroyed her on several occasions.

When I heard Greg's statement, I immediately thought about Bardon's soul mirror exercises. If Anna were to create her soul mirrors, would "ambition" go on her white soul mirror or her black soul mirror? If you've read the previous section, the answer is obvious. "Ambition" does not belong on either soul mirror because it is way too general. Anna should break this trait apart to find the smaller and more specific traits that constitute the bigger general traits. These smaller and more specific traits are what go on her soul mirrors. Some of them will go on her white soul mirror. Others will go on her black soul mirror.

<u>After Eating</u>

Ok, so you've impregnated your meal with charisma and then eaten it while focusing on the fact that you are consuming charisma. You've cleaned your plate. Are you done with conscious eating?

Most Bardonists would say yes, but believe it or not, you can extend this self-transformation technique to increase its effectiveness by adding a third phase to it. The three phases of the extended version of conscious eating are as follows:

Phase I: Impregnate the food with charisma.
Phase II: Eat the food while focusing on the fact that you are consuming charisma.
Phase III: After eating the food, focus on the fact that the food is permeating through your bodies (physical, astral, and mental) and being assimilated into them.

There are a number of ways you can do this third phase. After eating, you can just sit in a chair and feel the charisma permeating through your bodies and being assimilated into them. However, feel free to do other things too. For example, if you are a college student who has just finished lunch, you can begin preparing for your afternoon classes by taking your notebooks and papers for your morning classes out of your backpack, finding the notebooks and papers you need for your afternoon classes, and putting them into your backpack. While doing all of this, feel the charisma permeating through your bodies and being assimilated into them. Or, if you are a very disorganized person, you can spend some time organizing and tidying up your room. While doing this, feel the charisma permeating through your bodies and being assimilated into them.

You can even through some autosuggestion into this to further strengthen the techniques. For example, when you turn your attention to the feeling of the charisma permeating your bodies and being assimilated into them, you can repeat an affirmation like "I am charismatic."

Magical Washing Prior to Conscious Eating

If you're a busy person, you may be stressed by the time you sit down to eat lunch or dinner. Furthermore, there may be a many thoughts or worries in your mind. Your stress and your thoughts and worries can prevent you from concentrating when you impregnate your food and eat it. While washing your hands before eating, use magical washing to wash away your stress, as well as your thoughts and worries. Therefore, you will be relaxed and have a clear mind. In other words, you'll be in an ideal state to impregnate your food and focus on the fact that you are eating the quality you impregnated it with.

The Magical Exhalation

The magical exhalation can be used for the same purpose. Before eating, breathe out the stress that has accumulated in your body. In addition, breathe out the extraneous thoughts and worries in your mind.

While you are actually eating, you may find it a good idea to use a light magical exhalation every few bites or so to expel from yourself the mental chatter in your mind that is preventing you from focusing. Intermediate and advanced students of the Bardon system will see little reason in doing this, after all, they possess a good deal of mental discipline and their default mental state is one of peace and clarity anyway. However, if you are a beginning student, chances are that your default mental state is the so-called "monkey-mind" (overly-active and fickle) state. Therefore, as soon as you clear your mind by breathing out the thoughts that fill it, mental chatter will immediately begin to slowly build up in it again, so that every few minutes, you may need to clear your mind again with another magical exhalation until you are finished eating.

Conscious Eating While Tired

The effectiveness of conscious eating will not be as great if you do it when tired. If you feel tired, do something to bring yourself into a more alert and awake state. When you are an intermediate student, you should have enough control over yourself and your consciousness to do this at will. If you are a beginning student, you might need to splash your face with cold water, like Bardon suggests in IIH.

Present-Mindedness

The more skilled you are in concentration, the more effective conscious eating will be for you. Impregnating food involves concentration, as does focusing on the fact that you are consuming the quality when you eat it.

The second mental exercise of Step 1 is to focus on whatever you are doing. Regardless of whether you are driving to work, coding in MATLAB, flossing, cooking, or gardening, you do your best to remain completely focused on what you are doing. Needless to say, this practice greatly improves your ability to focus and concentrate. Therefore, it also improves the effectiveness of conscious eating for you.

Stay present-minded as often as possible. Don't let yourself become absent-minded or to allow daydreams and worries to consume your mind. Whatever you do, stay focused.

Music

In *The Spirit of Magic,* I mentioned that it is often necessary to make sacrifices if one is to advance along the magical path. I used to really like listening to music and would spend a lot of time doing it. Unfortunately, songs get stuck in my head very easily. Impregnating your food is a lot more difficult if there is a song stuck in your head; in fact, it is quite easy to accidentally impregnate the food with the song instead of with the quality you want to develop. As a result, I stopped listening to music for a large portion of my training to minimize the chances that a song would get stuck in my head and prevent me from concentrating well when I tried to impregnate my food.

The point of me sharing this anecdote isn't to imply that you should stop listening to music. It's to illustrate through example the fact that we need to make changes to our lives if we are to more efficiently make changes to our personalities.

What is Black Magic?

Little Mix's song "Black Magic" is interesting. Usually, when a potion is used for romance purposes, it is given to the object of one's affections so that he will drink it and fall in love with you. In the song, the situation is quite different. The potion is a consumable liquid that has been impregnated with confidence. The magician does not give this potion to the object of her affections, but consumes it herself. Upon consuming it, she develops the quality of confidence, which makes her much more desirable to the object of her affections and much more likely to capture his attention.

The following passage from the song's lyrics does exaggerate how quickly conscious eating/drinking works though.

Take a sip of my secret potion,

I'll make you fall in love.

For a spell that can't be broken,

One drop should be enough.

One drop/sip of an impregnated liquid is usually not enough to develop a quality. You usually need to impregnate your food and drink at every meal for a week or two before you begin noticing a change in your personality. However, once you have succeeded in developed confidence via conscious eating/drinking, it is true that the change is a "spell that can't be broken." The quality of confidence has become a real veritable part of your personality and is not a temporary illusion created through sorcery.

The Curiosity of Others

When you are skilled at conscious eating, you can impregnate your food pretty much instantaneously. This level of skill comes from a long period of practice and mental training. However, before you have acquired this level of skill, impregnating your food may require you to gaze at the food for a few moments while you impress charisma into its essence and will it to transform into charisma.

Needless to say, it is best to be as inconspicuous as possible when impregnating your food around others. In an ideal case, no one should notice you doing it. However, there is always the possibility that someone will notice you doing it and ask you a question like "Why are you staring at your food?"

Realize that you are under no obligation to give an explanation. Do you not have the right to stare at your food for a few moments before eating it? If you are gazing intently at your food and asked why you are doing this, an answer like "It's just something I do" or "Don't worry about it" should suffice. If you are pressed with further questions, these answers should be repeated.

For example...

Curious Observer: Why do you always spend time staring at your food before eating it?
Aspiring Magician: It's just something I do.
Curious Observer: Is there a reason?
Aspiring Magician: Not really. It's just something I do.
Curious Observer: If there's no reason to do it, you shouldn't do it.
Aspiring Magician: I'm sure that's true, but it's something I do?
Curious Observer: Are you going to stop doing it from now on?
Aspiring Magician: Probably not. It's just something I do.
Curious Observer: It seems to be a waste of time.
Aspiring Magician: That could be so, but it's just something I do.
Curious Observer: Do you have any idea how much time you could save in your life over the years if you didn't stare at your food for no reason before eating it?
Aspiring Magician: I don't know, but it's just something I do.
Curious Observer: Some people might feel uncomfortable about you staring at your food like that before eating it because it's kind of weird.
Aspiring Magician: That could be the case, but it's just something I do.

Needless to say, the above conversation depicts a worst-case scenario. I serious doubt you will ever encounter someone that nosy and obnoxious, but in the even that you do, remember the four power of the sphinx—"To Keep Silence." If someone notices you gazing at your food and asks you why you do that, don't panic and start rambling about how you are an aspiring magician who is trying to develop something called an "elemental equilibrium" so you can safely work with astra-mental energies and communicate with the denizens of the inner planes. That's not going to go well.

Absurd Scenario

Let's say someone notices you gazing at your food before eating it, walks up to you, points a gun at your head, and says "Give me a coherent explanation of why you gazed at your food for a few moments before eating it or I will shoot you." You don't want to tell him about your magical training, after all, that is none of his business and silence about one's magical practices is a potent catalyst for progress in one's magical training. What should you say?

I would recommend something like the following:

"I am practicing a spiritual exercise where I reflect on how fortunate I am to be able to eat and strive to develop gratitude for being able to eat. I believe this prevents me from taking life for granted or forgetting up how fortunate I am."

While this exact scenario might not happen, it's possible that you will encounter a scenario where you will feel that, for whatever reason, it is in your best interest to give an explanation.

The unpleasantness that comes from nosy people mentioned in this section and the previous section can be avoided if you become good at impregnating your food inconspicuously (yet effectively and thoroughly) in the presence of others.

I've never once encountered these types of issues. A couple of times, some good-natured people have seen me impregnating me food and asked me if I'm alright, but after saying something along the lines of "Yeah, I'm fine," they went away.[31]

Entering the Void

If you are proficient at entering the void, you may consider bringing the food with you into the void and impregnating it in there.

A detailed discussion of the void and the methods for entering the void is out of place here, but can be found in the writings of William Mistele and Josephine McCarthy. I will merely summarize the basic facts here.

The void is the infinite emptiness that contains everything in potential and from which all of creation arises.

There are several ways of entering the void. One way is through the use of the imagination. You begin by imagining your immediate surroundings (except the food) fading away. In other words, the objects around you, the walls surrounding you, the roof above you, and the ground beneath you fade away, leaving you suspended in outer space surrounded by stars. You then imagine the stars fading away. At the end of this process, you find yourself and the food in front of you suspended in the midst of an infinitely large void that extends in all direction. There is no matter, energy, or radiation in this void besides that which constitutes you and the food. The void is a place of perfect peace, serenity, calmness and stillness. This environment clears your mind and helps you focus. Therefore, you take advantage of this as you impregnate the food in front of you.

Needless to say, entering the void and bringing the food with you into it before impregnating it is far from necessary, but if you are proficient enough at entering the void that you can slip in and out of it at ease, you should consider experimenting with this idea to see if it enhances the effectiveness of conscious eating.

An Excerpt from Bill's Commentary

In Bill's commentary on IIH, he writes the following:

"In all of Bardon's exercises, it sometimes helps to imagine you have already mastered the exercise. This is an exercise in imagination. It gives you a chance to feel what it is like to do something you do not yet know how to do. And there is a sense that if you can imagine it then you can get it. The thought or image of already being able to do something creates energy which generates momentum and success."

These comments also apply to the conscious eating exercise. Imagine that you are a master of conscious eating. This will give you a taste of what it is like to be a master of conscious eating, and this taste will help guide you as you move in the direction of actually becoming a master of conscious eating.

In another one of his writings, Bill writes the following:

"Be aware that with a little imagination and focus we can recreate anything we have ever felt, will feel, or wish to feel."

True words indeed! With a little imagination and focus, you can create the sensation of possessing completely mastery over the technique of conscious eating (or conscious breathing, or magical washing, etc.).

<u>Incorrect Training</u>

I know a guy who wanted to get better at singing so he began practicing vocal exercises that would help his voice project and increase the range of his voice. Unfortunately, he didn't practice the exercises correctly and basically destroyed his vocal chords. If practiced correctly, those exercises would have made him a better singer. By practicing the exercises incorrectly, he only succeeded in injuring himself.

Many magical exercises, including conscious eating, are similar. If conscious eating is practiced correctly, it will help you establish an elemental equilibrium because you can use it to develop the traits you need in order to acquire a more balanced personality. However, if conscious eating is practiced incorrectly, it will cause you to injure yourself.

There are many ways one can incorrectly practice conscious eating. For example, people who try to impregnate food while they are angry inevitably end up impregnating the food with their anger instead of with the positive trait they want to develop. Needless to say, eating food impregnated with anger can have harmful consequences.

Eating More

The more impregnated food you eat, the more quickly you will develop the positive trait you desire to have. There is a wrong way and a right way to make practical use of this information.

The wrong way is to stuff yourself with as much food as possible during each meal. Trust me, the negative health effects that come from overeating three times a day will outweigh any benefits you could conceivably obtain from overeating instead of eating a moderate amount of food at each meal.

The right way is to impregnate the snacks you eat between meals. Most Bardonists practice conscious eating at breakfast, lunch, and dinner, but don't practice conscious eating when eating snacks between meals. Sometimes, it's because they snack while taking a break, and taking a break means giving both your mind as well as your body a break. Other times, it's because they snack while doing something that requires their attention, and so they cannot focus on the fact that they are consuming the quality they wish to develop. However, other times, it's because they are too lazy to. That's all fine. As long as you practice conscious eating at each meal, you will derive a lot of benefit from this technique.

However, if you snack frequently, I do encourage you to practice conscious eating while snacking as often as possible. It will increase rate at which the trait develops in your personality.

Medusa

People who looked at Medusa were turned into stone. They didn't become "filled" with stone. They didn't become "charged" with stone. They became stone.

Similarly, when you impregnate food with a quality, the food becomes that quality. It doesn't become "filled" with the quality. It doesn't become "charged" with the quality.

Indoor Magical Air Pollution

Let's say you are a stupid person and with to eliminate the quality of stupidity from yourself. You are sitting in a movie theater waiting for the movie to begin and decide to use the magical exhalation to do this. You take a deep breath and then exhale, breathing out all traces of stupidity from yourself as you do so. Great, now you are not stupid because you have breathed out your stupidity. However, those around you will breathe in the air you breathed out. Because that air is contaminated with stupidity, they will become stupid. When you use the magical exhalation to breathe out a negative trait, you contaminate the air around you with that negative trait.

There are two solutions to this. The first is to use the power of focused intent to clean the air immediately after you are breathing it out. For example, if you breathe out stupidity, you would then use the power of focused intent to transmute the air into pure clean air that is not contaminated by stupidity.

The second solution is to move the contamination outside of the building. The air is physical, so obviously you cannot use focused intent to move the air outside. However, the air possesses a certain quality, and this quality is the quality of being contaminated with stupidity. You can take this quality and move it from the air inside to the air outside.

It may seem tiring to use focused intent to magical purify the air you breathe out each time you use the magical exhalation indoors. This is why I usually use the magical exhalation outdoors. When you breathe out a negative quality outdoors, the air quickly becomes diluted to the point where it won't negatively affect anyone if they breathe it in.

I usually only use the magical exhalation indoors if I am in a room with an open window so the contaminated air can flow out the window.

Seeds

In Jan Fries's book *Visual Magick*, he writes the following about seeds:

"A seed is a unit of consciousness that has body, charge, and intelligence and tends to develop from potential into the actual under proper conditions. Seeds are created, transmitted, and earthed in order to achieve change—change in one's world, life, or identity."

The affirmation you recite when you use autosuggestion is a seed. Each time you repeat the affirmation, you send a seed into your subconscious in the hopes that it will change your personality by growing into a personality trait.

Viewing affirmations as seeds gets the aspiring magician to ask many important questions. Not all seeds grow, so how can you be sure that the seeds you plant in your subconscious mind will grow?

For a seed to grow, it must be nurtured and the plant it grows into must be cared for. Similarly, as the seed in your subconscious grows into a personality trait, the trait must be nurtured. Let's say that you repeat the affirmation "I am charismatic." It takes root deep within you and grows into the trait of charisma. When you eat food impregnated with charisma and inhale air impregnated with charisma, this food and air can be seen as fertilizer for the new plant. There are many things (viruses, insects, weeds, etc.) that will attack the plant and try to kill it. For example, traits like insecurity, social anxiety, and shyness will try to prevent charisma from growing inside of you. You remove these by expelling them using the magical exhalation or by using magical washing to wash them out of you.

As far as the subject of seeds and self-transformation goes, I will leave you with one of my favorite sayings. Several versions exist that all differ slightly in their wording, but the version I like best is as follows.

"Don't worry if your tasks are small or if rewards are few. Remember that the mighty oak was once a nut like you."

Bits and Pieces Cut from *The Covert Side of Initiation*

Fighting and Struggling

Some people view life as just one fight or struggle after another. Getting out of bed in the morning is a fight. Getting yourself to eat healthy food instead of junk food involves a fight with temptation. When you are in school, you fight to get good grades. Once you are out of school, you fight to make money. You fight to pay off your mortgage. You fight to ensure your kids have a good future. Since everything in life is a fight, if you're not willing to fight, or if you don't have what it takes to fight, then you will never get anything done, or so it seems.

Since one's magical training is integrated into one's life, it's no surprise that many people view the magical path as one filled with fights and magical training as just one fight after another. When you practice present-mindedness, you fight to keep your attention on the present moment. When you practice concentration, you fight to keep your attention on whatever you are concentrating on. When you practice VOM, you keep your mind empty by fighting off any thoughts that try to enter it. When you visualize an object and it keeps dancing around, you fight to keep it still. You fight against your negative traits. You fight to make time for your magical exercises each day. To these people, it's all about fighting. Viewing magical training as just a series of fights isn't a new fad. This perspective on the process has been around for years. That's why a lot of magical texts obsess over willpower. Just as physical strength will help you win in a literal physical fight, willpower will help you win in any metaphorical fight, like the fight to keep the visualized object still, or the fight against the intruding thoughts that try to disrupt your vacancy of mind, or the fight to wake up early so you can practice your magical exercise.

The magician should develop a sense of well-being. I wrote about this in Chapter 6. If everything you do in your life is a fight or struggle, you're not going to have a sense of well-being. Does this mean the magician should sit in his room all day without doing anything? No, a magician is an active and productive individual. The key to working productively and getting a lot done without struggling can be found in the story of Cook Ting and Lord Wenhui (Google this and go read it now).

For most cooks, cutting an ox is a struggle. If a cook doesn't want to struggle, he can choose not to cut an ox, but then he is not being productive and just wasting time. Cook Ting, however, cuts the ox, but because of the way he cuts the ox, it's not a struggle for him and he doesn't need a lot of strength. In order to be productive, you need to accomplish a lot of tasks. If you approach each task the way Cook Ting approached cutting the ox, then none of the tasks will be a struggle. They might be challenging, but they won't be a struggle. In this way, you can be very productive while still maintaining a sense of well-being.

Strive to approach each task in your magical path the way Cook Ting approached cutting the ox. The better you are at this, the less struggle will be involved in your magical training.

Your Life is Yours

An acquaintance and I once visited a library together. He took several books off the shelves to flip through, and when he was done, he shoved them back onto the shelf at random locations. I was appalled at this behavior and asked him why he didn't put the books back in their proper locations. He explained to me that because he didn't own the bookshelf, he didn't care about keeping it organized. Since it belonged to the library and not to him, he figured it was the library's responsibility to keep the shelf organized, not his. This incident gave me some insight into why some people never get their lives organized.

Some people don't get their lives organized because they think it's the government's job to do that, or it's society's job to do that, or it's their parent's job to do that. The government doesn't own your life. Society doesn't own your life. Your parents don't own your life. You own your life. Therefore, it's your responsibility to keep it organized and clean. It's when we reject responsibility for our own lives that our lives begin falling apart.

Some people throw trash everywhere on the ground at their workplace, expecting custodians to pick it up. They don't own the building. The company they work for owns the building. Therefore, they have no qualms about making a mess in it. They feel that it's the company's job to clean up messes in their building. Again, it's appalling behavior, but it shows that in general, people are more willing to take responsibility for things they perceive to be their own, and to not worry about the state of things they perceive as belonging to others.

At the very beginning of your self-transformation journey, you must accept that you and you alone are responsible for your personality and your life.

A World of Possibilities

Once you transform yourself for the better, a whole world of new possibilities and opportunities opens up for you. Right now, you probably cannot conceive of its enormous magnitude.

Let's say you are an elementary school student who is really lazy. You always get bad grades because you are too lazy to study or do your homework. There's a good chance you will drop out of high school and never get a college education. However, if you transform yourself so that you are hard-working, then suddenly it becomes much more likely you will graduate high school and get a college degree. This will enable you to pursue numerous career paths that were previously hard to reach. Just by developing one trait, many great opportunities were made available to you.

Let's say that you are addicted to smoking. If you eliminate your addiction to smoking, there is a good chance you will significantly extend your lifespan. With more time in your life, you have the opportunity to do more, see more, and be more. All of this increased fulfillment in life comes from eliminating just one trait.

How to Learn More About Yourself

The more different things you do, the more you will learn about yourself. Swami Sivananda talks about a man who thought he had eliminated the trait of irritability within himself. He lived in a cave and avoided contact with humans. As a result, he never met anyone who made him angry, and therefore, he didn't know that he possessed the trait of irritability. If the man had gone to a nearby village, he would have encountered numerous annoying people who would have triggered his irritability, causing it to produce the emotion of anger within him.

Many times, your personality traits give rise to an emotion when triggered. When your irritability is triggered, perhaps by someone insulting you, then the emotion known as anger is produced within you. When your lustfulness is triggered, perhaps by a pornographic image, then the emotion known as lust is produced within you. When your impatience is triggered, perhaps by a traffic jam, then the emotion known as frustration is produced within you. See how these personality traits are triggered by various experiences you undergo or things you encounter? If you never encountered anything that would make you angry, in other words nothing that would trigger your irritability, you would have no way of knowing whether or not you possess the trait of irritability. As you can see, undergoing numerous diverse experiences and encounters is highly conducive to learning more about your personality.

True Changes in Personality

Let's say you possess an addiction to smoking. You could use willpower to force yourself to stop smoking. This doesn't mean that you have eliminated the addiction from yourself. The fact that you need to apply effort to force yourself to refrain from smoking is proof that the negative trait is still there. The more effort you need to apply, the stronger the trait is. When you no longer need to apply any effort to refrain from smoking, then the trait has been eliminated. Normally, willpower alone is not enough to eliminate a deeply rooted trait like an addiction. You need to use other methods, for example the magical exhale to exhale out the addiction, and the use of the magic of water to wash away the addiction.

This applies to other traits. Let's say that you have made an effort to act generously and succeeded in doing this for a day. This is a good start, but that's all it is. It doesn't mean you have developed the trait of generosity. When you act generously without needing to make an effort to, then you will have developed the trait of generosity.

Plan for Eliminating a Negative Trait

The following steps can be taken to eliminate a negative trait.

1. Definitively decide to eliminate that negative trait, and to work persistently toward eliminating that trait until you are successful.
2. Carry out the analysis process of analyzing the trait described in the previous section.
3. Do some research on the trait.
4. Begin applying the six-pronged attack to eliminate the trait.
5. Fake it till you make it.
6. Keep a journal documenting your progress in eliminating the trait.

In a previous book, I wrote about the importance of clearly defining your goals, and how this is an important step towards actually achieving your goals. Your goal is to eliminate the negative trait. Write this goal down on paper. Write down something like "I will work steadily and persistently to eliminate impatience from myself and become patient." Actually writing this sentence out by hand ingrains into your mind the fact that you are serious about this work. It sends a message to your subconscious mind that says "Yes, I am doing this. It's going to happen."

For the third step, start by searching the trait on Google and reading some articles about it. Seek to get an understanding of the trait, its possible sources of origin, its potential negative effects on your life, and suggestions for eliminating it or keeping it under control. If you want, you can also visit a library and check out some books on the subject. The library nearest to me has a whole shelf full of books on anger and anger-management. Write down any information you find to be particularly useful or insightful.

The six-pronged attack is described in my book *The Elemental Equilibrium: Notes on the Foundation of Magical Adepthood*. It consists of using autosuggestion, conscious eating, conscious breathing, the magic of water, willpower, and various non-magical methods to eliminate a negative trait (or develop a positive trait).

In the fifth step, you live your life as if you did not possess the negative trait you are trying to rid yourself of. For example, if you are trying to rid yourself of impatience, then you live your life acting as if you were a patient person. This is actually a part of the third step. It is the use of the volition prong.

In the sixth step, you write about your endeavor to eliminate the trait from yourself. No, this is not a "magic journal." It's just a journal. There is no formal structure for entries that you need to adhere to. No, you don't need to write in it every day. No, you don't need to write down everything in it. I would suggest writing down your major failures and successes. Describe them. For the failures, if you can identify a reason for your failure, then write down that reason. Also, make a note telling yourself (in the imperative) not to repeat the mistake. Use affirmative wording.

Uniqueness

At the core of everyone's being is a divine spark. Divinity is balanced because it is omnipotent (fire), omniscient (air), omnipresent (water), and eternal (earth). The idea behind an elemental equilibrium is that your astra-mental body reflects the quality of your inner divine nature. Since your inner divine nature is balanced, your astra-mental body needs to be balanced for this to happen. Since your personality is a function of your astra-mental body, this will result in a balanced personality. Some people think that if everyone has an elemental equilibrium, then everyone will be the same. The opposite is true. Everyone's divine spark is different and unique, and therefore, if everyone has an elemental equilibrium, everyone's personality will be different and unique.

It is because people lack an elemental equilibrium that they lose their uniqueness. When you do not have an elemental equilibrium, you are easily influenced. Commercials designed to convince you that you need to wear a specific brand of clothing to be a respectable citizen will likely succeed. When people try to peer pressure you into doing something, they are likely to succeed. You will be at the mercy of the astral currents that flow through society and manifest as various trends, movements, and fashions. Often, people want to jump on the bandwagon. Instead of remaining true to who they are, they do what others do, wear what others wear, and act the way others act. Your personality influences the way you act, but the way you act also influences your personality. This road of influence goes both ways. If you act like everyone else, your personality will become more like everyone else. It's not that you lose your uniqueness, but that your uniqueness becomes buried under a corrupted artificial personality that you likely identify with.

To have an elemental equilibrium is to be truly unique. Never lose sight of this fact and its implications.

Five Things You Should Know About Communicating With Your Subconscious Mind

1. Send positive messages to your subconscious mind. This is why Bardon says to avoid falling asleep in a bad mood, but there are many other ways besides that in which you can send negativity to your subconscious mind.

2. Appreciate your subconscious mind. Realize that it exists to help and support you, but that sometimes it needs direction and instruction from your conscious mind. Any form of suggestion, such as autosuggestion, can be used to provide that direction and instruction to your subconscious mind, however, for your subconscious mind to understand your directions and instructions, they must be worded in the language of your subconscious mind.

3. When communicating with your subconscious mind, speak the language of your subconscious mind.[32]

4. Realize that a variety of ways to sending suggestions to your subconscious mind exist. For example, if you are trying to send a suggestion to your subconscious mind that you are successful, autosuggestion is one way. You can use autosuggestion to send the suggestion by repeating the affirmation "I am successful." However, successful people are organized, and unsuccessful people are disorganized. The senses are the gateways to the inner layers of oneself. If your house is disorganized, then you will see this when you look around. This will cause the suggestion that you are unorganized (and therefore unsuccessful) to be sent to your subconscious mind via the gateway that is the sense of sight.

5. Communication with your subconscious mind is not just about sending messages to your subconscious mind. It's also about receiving and heeding the messages your subconscious mind sends to you. Learning to listen to the messages of your subconscious mind (which usually come via intuition) will make it easier to send messages to your subconscious mind.[33] Communication goes both ways.

Ten Things Bardonists on Step 2 Should Know About Self-Transformation

1. You need to desire to change yourself from the bottom of your heart. You can't just kind of want to change yourself. You need to be completely serious about transforming yourself and determined to carry out this work no matter what obstacles stand in your way.

2. Self-transformation should be fun and enjoyable.

3. Some negative traits will take you a very short time to get rid of, but other negative traits will take you a very long time to get rid of. Don't be discouraged when that happens. As long as you work persistently to get rid of the trait, you will eventually succeed.

4. There are no shortcuts when it comes to self-transformation. If some occultist tries to sell you a ritual or potion that he claims can instantly make you into a much better person or instantly give you an elemental equilibrium, that occultist is running a scam.

5. The work of self-transformation does not end once you've completed Step 2. In fact, it never ends. You will continue this work every day of your life.

6. Many other Bardonists have successfully transformed themselves for the better when working through Step 2 and have been able to move on to Step 3 as a result. If they can do it, so can you.

7. You must know yourself first before you can effectively transform yourself. To know yourself, create a set of soul mirrors.

8. Transforming yourself for the better won't just improve your own life. It will also improve the life of anyone who is close to you or interacts with you. This fact can be used

as a source of motivation in your self-transformation work. If you won't do it for yourself, then do it for your loved ones.

9. Self-transformation is a gradual process. Don't start off by trying to force yourself to be a perfect person living a perfect life.

10. I wrote a book on self-transformation. It's called *The Elemental Equilibrium: Notes on the Foundation of Magical Adepthood*.

Discrimination

Discrimination is one of the first skills that the aspiring magician must learn. At the very beginning of his path, he must discriminate between valid systems of magic and invalid systems of magic. Amongst the valid systems of magic, he must discriminate between those that resonate well with him and those that don't. He must discriminate between books that are worth reading and books that aren't. He must discriminate between the good advice he receives and the bad advice he receives. He must discriminate between the good personality traits he possesses and the bad personality traits he possesses.

Constructive Criticism

The esoteric world is filled with wonderful spiritual principles that numerous people study but don't apply. One of these is the idea that the Pillar of Mercy must always be balanced by the Pillar of Severity.

Not too long ago, I made a comment online in which I listed some ways in which a particular magical training system is incomplete. In reply to my comment, someone accused me of "condemning" this system. Again, all I did was point out some ways that the system is incomplete.

Pointing out the ways in which that magical training system is incomplete was my way of offering constructive criticism in regards to that system. The response to my comment, however, revealed to me a glaring problem in the esoteric world. Many esotericists believe that being a nice person is a sign of spiritual development and maturity. They're absolutely right; however, being a nice person doesn't mean refraining from offering constructive criticism. Too many esotericists don't realize there is a difference between constructive criticism, which is helpful to the receiver, and the insults and slander that are designed to tear down a target.

Constructive criticism, as its name implies, is designed to help construct, or build up, something. A personal attack is designed to destroy something. If you read my writings often, you know that I like to think of magic as a form of engineering.

Imagine a university with a mechanical engineering program. Any solid mechanical engineering program will have a fluid mechanics course in its curriculum. A lack of a fluid mechanics course in a mechanical engineering curriculum indicates that the curriculum is not complete. Let's say that this university's mechanical engineering curriculum does not have a fluid mechanics course. The people who graduate with degrees in mechanical engineering from this university won't be qualified to do their job. Mechanical engineers do a lot of work with airplanes. Air is a fluid, so knowledge of fluid mechanics is necessary to understand how the flow of air interacts with and affects the various components of an airplane. A graduate from the university who tries to get a job working on airplanes could make serious errors. This could result in a great loss of life. Obviously, this is bad for a lot of people. It's bad for the families of those who lost their lives in the airplane accident. It's bad for the mechanical engineer because he feels guilty that his low quality work resulted in a lot of people getting killed. It's also bad for the university because its graduates will look incompetent (because they are). Thus, a degree from that university will be worth very little.

If you were the head of the mechanical engineering department at this university, you would obviously want information about how the mechanical engineering curriculum is incomplete. Giving this information is an example of constructive criticism. It's intended to help build up the curriculum and make it better. If you gave the department head accurate information about how the curriculum is incomplete, he would not accuse you of "condemning" his curriculum or making a personal attack on it. He would thank you.

Let's go back to the esoteric principle that asserts the importance of constructive criticism. This principle is that the Pillar of Mercy must be balanced with the Pillar of Severity.

The Pillar of Mercy is the pillar of praise. Let's say you create a system of magical training. I can sit around all day and praise the good parts of the system. This is helpful because it tells you what parts of the system you don't need to change. However, it's not enough feedback from me if you want the system to be as good as possible. For that, you need the Pillar of Severity, which is the pillar of constructive criticism. If I provide constructive criticism by pointing out the bad parts of the system, then you can fix those bad parts in order to improve the system. In this way, we see that excellent feedback has elements from both the Pillar of Mercy and the Pillar of Severity. At certain specific times, you might want one or the other—praise or constructive criticism. However, by the time you are finished creating the system and finalizing its curriculum, you need to have received both.

The Myth of the Magical Path

The idea of a "magical path" is a prominent one in the modern magical world. I use this idea frequently in this book, as well as my other books. In my first book, for example, there is a chapter called "Walking the Path." The "magical path" metaphor/analogy compares magical training to walking along a path. It's not a bad metaphor/analogy, but like any metaphor/analogy, it's not perfect. In this section, I want to examine why it's not perfect. It turns out that if you think this metaphor/analogy is more perfect than it actually is, you can use it as an excuse to waste large amounts of time. Some people even waste their whole lives, and then use the "magical path" metaphor/analogy to trick themselves into thinking they were productive. Thus, they don't feel bad. Their ability to trick themselves in this manner is wholly dependent on the assumption that the "magical path" metaphor/analogy is perfect. Again, it is not.

The basic idea of the "magical path" metaphor/analogy is that every person has his own unique path to adepthood. For example, imagine a mountain. At the top of the mountain is adepthood. Everyone starts at the bottom of the mountain and walks to the top. Everyone finds their own unique path up to the top.

This is wrong. Search all around on the mountain and you will not find a unique path that will lead you to the top. This is because there are no paths at all on the mountain. Therefore, instead of focusing on trying to find a path to the top of the mountain, focus on trying to get to the top of the mountain.

A lot of people go about magical training in a highly ineffective manner. When they are told this, they explain that they are just following their own path, and that because you are not them, you are not qualified to comment on their path or criticize their path. While they are correct that you are not qualified to criticize their approach to magical training, their reasoning behind asserting this is incorrect because there are no paths. Therefore, there is no path to comment on or criticize.

To become an adept, you need to walk to the top of the mountain. As long as you are doing something related to magic, you are walking. If you are working through IIH step by step, you are walking. If you are working through the Golden Dawn system grade by grade, you are walking. If you dabble a little bit in one system for a week and then dabble in another system for another week and continue to dabble in a new system every week, you are walking. However, just because you are walking doesn't mean you are walking up the mountain. A lot of people are walking in circles. Others are walking in the wrong direction. Others walk in every direction but the direction of the mountaintop.

If we compare magical advancement to walking up a mountain, then a magical system is like a compass that is supposed to point to the top of the mountain.[34] A compass does not tell you how to take every step. It just provides guidance by pointing you in the right direction. Magical training systems are the same way. When you first begin your magical training, IIH will tell you the right direction—the direction of becoming aware of your thoughts, learning to introspect, and taking measures to improve yourself. It won't tell you how to take every step along the way. If you encounter an obstacle, it won't tell you how to get past it. Let's say there is an obstacle consisting of a lack of time. This obstacle prevents you from going in the direction that IIH points you toward —the direction of becoming aware of your thoughts, learning to introspect, and taking measures to improve yourself. You have to figure out how to overcome the obstacle yourself so you can actually go in that direction.

If a magical training system is valid, it will in fact point to the top of the mountain. If it's not a valid magical system, it won't. I know of a compass that points to the top of the mountain. I also know of a compass that points in the wrong direction, a compass that is missing a needle, and a compass with a needle that is constantly spinning in circles. I also know of a compass that is actually a cheeseburger. For some reason, people think it's a compass but it's not.

Some people refuse to pick a system of magical training. They take pride in "not tying themselves down." Thus, they dabble in a new magical system or tradition each week. They do whatever they feel like. This is akin to someone on the mountain who goes north when he feels like going north, goes south when he feels like going south, goes east when he feels like going east, and goes west when he feels like going west. Such a person will never reach the top of the mountain.

There are two aspects of human nature—the divine aspect and the animal aspect. The divine aspect is represented by the woman in the Strength card. The animal aspect is represented by the lion in that same card. *The Magical Ritual of the Sanctum Regnum* contains a chapter about each card in the Major Arcana. In the chapter about the Strength card, Eliphas Levi writes that "To live a life guided by the caprice of the moment is to lead the life of an animal; this may conceivably be a life of innocence, but it is a life of submission." Some people think that "tying themselves down" to a system makes them submissive, and thus, to avoid leading a life of submission, they refuse to do so. This is ironic. Dabbling in a new system or tradition whenever you feel like it is leading a life of submission. You are entirely the slave of the caprice of the moment. To dabble in whatever you want whenever you want shows a complete lack of discipline. The animal side of man, like any wild animal, possesses no self-discipline. To stick to one system of magical training requires self-discipline. This is not a submissive life, after all, no one who possesses self-discipline can be said to be submissive. In many ways, a person's level of liberation is directly proportional to how much self-discipline he possesses. A valid system of magical training helps one progress in one's training, and progress in magical training is in part a process of liberation. Thus, by trying to avoid a life of submission, dabblers are avoiding the single biggest tool available that can free them from the life of submission they are already living—genuine initiation.

Think of the process of creating a path through a forest. For this to happen, many people walk a route through the forest. Their feet wear away the vegetation, leaving a clearly marked path of compressed dirt. In the process, they also remove any obstacles like fallen trees. If they come across a big obstacle like a boulder, they go around it. They avoid the dangerous areas of a forest. Thus, when the path is finished, it does not run through any dangerous areas and there are no obstacles on the path. Also, there is no uncertainty because the path is clearly marked. This is another reason that a path is not a perfect metaphor, because you may encounter obstacles and dangers on your way to adepthood. In addition, you will encounter lots of uncertainty.

Let's say three people use the IIH compass. Their names are Sam, Mia, and Emily. All of them start at the bottom of the mountain. Sam starts on the eastern side of the mountain. Mia starts on the western side of the mountain. Emily starts on the northern side of the mountain. All of them start at the bottom.

Sam starts walking up the mountain with her compass guiding her. She comes across a lake. The compass tells her she needs to go forward, but the lake is blocking her. The compass does not tell her how to build a boat. However, she manages to figure out how to build a boat, then builds one and rows over the lake. She then walks onward and reaches the top of the mountain.

Mia starts walking up the mountain with her compass guiding her. She comes across a big rock and can't go around it. She spends a week lifting smaller rocks to build up her muscles and then lifts the big rock up so she can go under it. She then proceeds onward to the top of the mountain.

Emily starts walking up the mountain with her compass guiding her. She comes across a tiger that won't let her pass. She spends a week learning kung fu, then fights and defeats the tiger. She then proceeds onward to the top of the mountain.

Sam, Mia, and Emily are all at the top of the mountain. They've all completed their training in IIH, and therefore, they all know how to condense and project energy, exteriorize their mental bodies, enter an akashic trance, and transplant their consciousness into external objects. However, each of them has also acquired some unique skills and abilities that the others didn't. Sam knows how to make a boat. Mia is really strong. Emily knows kung fu. They have these different skills and abilities because they encountered different obstacles and problems on their way to adepthood.

With some spiritual traditions, all the followers think the same way and do the same things. They're all clones of each other. IIH isn't like that. Despite the fact that all Bardonists practice the same exercises, if you examine the adepts of the system, you see extraordinary diversity. Some people are college students when they start working through IIH. Some people are single mothers without a high school diploma. Others are CEOs in their mid-forties. Some are rich. Some are poor. Some are busy. Some have a lot of free time. We all start at a different place when we take the first step—Step 1. That step is very similar for all of us. It's just a matter of putting one foot in front of the other. However, taking that step will bring some of us face to face with a lake. It will bring others face to face with a giant rock. It will bring others face to face with a tiger. It brings different people face to face with different obstacles. Some people might take that first step and not encounter any obstacle at all. However, everyone encounters obstacles at some point in their training. We all encounter different obstacles. We all acquire different bits of knowledge, different traits, and different skills in the process of overcoming these different obstacles. Thus, when we reach the top of the mountain, we are very different from the others at the top, even though we all used the same compass.

The mountain you climb is a function of the world. As a simple example, let's say that the world is filled with smog, and the health effects on your lungs have a negative impact on your training. This is an obstacle you face as you walk towards adepthood. If the world wasn't filled with smog, you wouldn't face this obstacle. The world is constantly changing. Therefore, the mountain is constantly changing. The mountain that the Bardonists of today climb will not be the same as the mountain the Bardonists fifty years from now will climb. The world will be different, so the mountain will have different obstacles scattered through it. The compass, which is the Bardon system, will stay the same and always point to the top.

Evangelism

There's no room for evangelism in magic. Magicians work to improve the world. We want to see the world transformed into a more blessed, joyful, and wonderful version of itself. This isn't a one-man job. The more magicians there are working on this, the better. If someone completes his magical training via IIH, becoming a Bardon-trained magician, that's a big win for all Bardon-trained magicians. If someone completes his magical training via a different system, then that is an equally big win for all Bardon-trained magicians.

This is why, if a person is looking for a solid system of magical training that can help him become an adept, you should not try to convince him to work through the Bardon system. You should convince him to work through the system of magical training that resonates the best with him and his life. This is the system that will help him become a full-fledged magician the fastest. Thus, as a magician, it's in your best interest for him to pick the system best suited for him.

You can encourage him to check out the Bardon system and explain why it is worth checking out, and you can provide him with information about the Bardon system to help him see whether or not it resonates well with him, but don't try to convince him to ultimately choose the Bardon system as his system. That is a decision only he is qualified to make, and he needs to make it based on his own reasoning and intuition, without being influenced by others who do not know him and his life as well as he does.

Know Thyself

For years, esoteric teaches have told their students "Know thyself." Since the magical disciplines form a subset of the esoteric disciplines, magical teachers and systems have also told their students "Know thyself." Is this a good idea? I'm not so sure it is. Just telling students of magic to "Know thyself" gives them the impression that he is to know himself for the sake of knowing himself.

As far as magic goes, it is better for students to take to heart the phrase "Know yourself and then make use of the knowledge you have of yourself" rather than just "Know thyself." In Step 1, you work to know yourself by making your soul mirrors. Do you stop there? No. In Step 2 you put that knowledge to practical use. Because you know what your negative traits are, you can work to rid yourself of them.

When it comes to western spirituality, "Know thyself" is a traditional teaching. "Know yourself and then make use of the knowledge you have of yourself" is not a traditional teaching. However, it is not important that students of magic receive traditional teachings, but that they receive accurate and useful teachings. Knowledge is power, but if you're not going to use power, you might as well not have it. The process of acquiring knowledge of yourself and the process of using the knowledge you have of yourself are deeply intertwined with each other, and deeply intertwined with every step along any genuine magician's path.

Works Cited, Referenced, or Consulted

Bardon, Franz. *Initiation into Hermetics: A Course of Instruction of Magic Theory and Practice*. Wuppertal, Western Germany: D. Rüggeberg, 1987. Print.

Bardon, Franz. *The Key to the True Quabbalah: The Quabbalist as a Sovereign in the Microcosm and the Macrocosm*. Wuppertal, Western Germany: D. Rüggeberg, 1986. Print.

Bardon, Franz. *The Practice of Magical Evocation: Instructions for Invoking Spirits from the Spheres Surrounding Us*. Wuppertal, W. Germany: D. Rüggeberg, 1991. Print.

Clark, Rawn. "A Bardon Companion." *A Bardon Companion*. A Bardon Companion, 2014. Web. 12 June 2016.

Fries, Jan. *Visual Magick: a Practical Guide to Trance, Sigils and Visualization Techniques*. Mandrake, 2007.

Gundarsson, Kveldulf. *Teutonic Magic: The Magical and Spiritual Practices of the Germanic Peoples*. Llewellyn Publications, 1990.

Levi, Eliphas, and W. Wynn Westcott. "The Magical Ritual of the Sanctum Regnum." (2009): n. pag. *The Magical Ritual of the Sanctum Regnum*. Hermetics.org, 21 July 2000. Web. 12 June 2016.

Levi, Eliphas. *Transcendental Magic*. Newburyport: Red Wheel Weiser, 1968. Print.

McCarthy, Josephine. *Magical Knowledge Book II: The Initiate*. Mandrake of Oxford, 2011.

Markides, Kyriacos C. *The Magus of Strovolos*. Penguin Books, 1985.

McCarthy, Josephine. *Quareia the Apprentice: Book One*. Quareia Publishing, 2015

Mistele, William. "Franz Bardon Hermetics, Fairy Tales, and Transpersonal Psychology." *Bardon Home Page*. William Mistele, n.d. Web. 12 June 2016.

Nichols, Michael P. *The Lost Art of Listening*. The Guilford Press, 1995.

O'Donohue, John. *Anam Cara*. Cliff Street Books, 1997

Ransome, Arthur. *"The Fool of the World and the Flying Ship." Old Peter's Russian Tales: The Fool of the World and the Flying Ship, Sacred Texts,* www.sacred-texts.com/neu/oprt/oprt07.htm.

Rodenburg, Patsy. *The Second Circle: How to Use Positive Energy for Success in Every Situation*. W.W. Norton & Company, 2008

Sivananda. *Conquest of Anger*. Yoga-Vedanta Forest Academy, 1962.

Smith, Manuel J. *When I Say No, I Feel Guilty: How to Cope Using the Skills of Systematic Assertive Therapy*. The Dial Press, 1975.

The Holy Bible: New International Version. Zondervan, 2017.

1. http://williammistele.com/essays.html
2. http://williammistele.com/tenrules.htm
3. http://williammistele.com/tenrules1.pdf
4. https://theomagica.com/blog/2011/5/10/three-keys-to-magic-or-why-the-f-did-this-insight-take-so-lo.html
5. Everything I write about speech in this chapter applies not just to physical speech with the voice, but to online speech on forums and social media as well.
6. Well, it often is. If you're planning a surprise birthday party for a friend and need to lie to him to keep it a secret from him, then there's nothing wrong with that. I'm referring to lies told because of shady or ignoble motives.
7. NN was a well-known politician running for office at the time.
8. The Six-Pronged Attack is as follows:
    1. Autosuggestion
    2. Conscious eating
    3. Conscious breathing
    4. Magical washing
    5. Volition
    6 Non-magical methods
9. You can also breathe out your absentmindedness, your tendency to become distracted, and your tendency to daydream at inappropriate times.
10. If after trying this for a week or so you feel it is effective, you can consider writing the written imperative down more often. For example, whenever you have free time, take out the notebook and write it down a few times.
11. See the conversation with the archdemon in the Tiphereth chapter of TRFSS(EV).
12. A macroscopic strategy is designed to encompass a time period lasting around several weeks. A microscopic strategy is designed to encompass a time period lasting around several minutes.
13. http://williammistele.com/focusing.html
14. http://users.rider.edu/~suler/zenstory/moon.html
15. http://www.sacred-texts.com/neu/oprt/oprt07.htm
    There are numerous magical lessons to be taken from this fairy tale. The person who got the princess was a fool. That is to say, he was in shoshin.
16. http://williammistele.com/cigila
17. http://williammistele.com/saturn2.html
18. There are many articles that discuss the trap of rationalization. A simple Google search will turn up a lot of good ones. The Wikipedia article about rationalization isn't a bad place to start researching it if you want to understand the trap in order to better avoid it.
    https://en.wikipedia.org/wiki/Rationalization_(psychology)
19. Honestly, a chapter on dealing with your fears belongs in this book but I don't feel I'm qualified to write such a chapter so I haven't. If you approach the process of dealing with your fears incorrectly, you can really mess yourself up. I don't want anyone to mess themselves up because of something I said. Go to Frater Acher's site (Theomagica) and type "fear" in the search bar.

Also, Google "site:williammistele.com fear". This, in addition to the chapter in *The Second Circle,* should provide you with enough initial reading material.

20 http://angelichealing.net/ali_spared.html

21 There is a prayer in some grimoire I read many years ago that began "Lord God Almighty, Creator and Maker of Heaven and Earth." For some reason I've always began my prayers that way since reading it. I was trying to locate the exact prayer so I could cite it but am unable to. There are prayers in the *Ars Notoria* with similar beginnings and there is a prayer in the *Arbatel of Magic* with a similar beginning, but I haven't been able to find the one with that exact beginning.

22 The word "bad" might seem like a general term, but I need a general term because the ways in which consuming junk esoteric writings can have a negative impact on you are wide and varied.

23 "Know thyself"

24 "Nothing in excess"

25 Reading Exercise 1: Read Aimee Bender's short story "End of the Line." What are some indications that while the big man is physically big, he's not actually that big (e.g. not going to Paris despite buying the ticket, the woman's reaction when he tried to ask her out, etc.). After doing this, reflect on the ways in which you are similar to the big man and contemplate courses of action you can take to become less like the big man. Why does the small woman feel pity for the big man in the last line of the story?

26 See Harry Mills's book *Artful Persuasion*. I forget the exact companies that were involved, but one of them was told by their lawyers to make eye contact with the jurors, smile at them, and joke with them. The other company was told to avoid making eye contact and to have a serious demeanor in order to show that they were serious people. The jurors interpreted the lack of eye contact and serious expressions of that company's representatives as indications of guilt, and the eye contact and openness of the other company as indications that they had nothing to hide. Part of being charismatic is making good eye contact with others, smiling genuine smiles, and using humor to liven up situations. So, the representatives of the company that won were essentially just told to be charismatic. Charisma on Command has some great videos on making eye contact, smiling genuine smiles, and using humor to get people to like you.

27 Don't try to be aware. Definitely don't try too hard to be aware. Just be aware.

28 The first mental exercise in Step 1 is to observe the thoughts in your mind. The third mental exercise is to hold just one thought in your mind.
Holding the thought "All nations are at peace with each other" in your mind is not the same as visualizing all nations being at peace with each other or mentally repeating the phrase "All nations are at peace with each other." It is impossible to describe in words what it means to hold a thought in your mind, but if you are truly proficient in the first mental exercise, you should know perfectly well what this means.

29 http://williammistele.com/body1.htm

30 It's a bit like trying to explain color to a blind person.
31 From what I can gather, I have an intense expression on my face when I impregnate my food, so they probably thought I was disturbed or upset about something. They meant no harm and were being compassionate, not nosy.
32 http://williammistele.com/astral2.html
33 Messages from your subconscious mind actually originate in your higher self, but pass through your subconscious mind in order to reach your conscious mind.
34 As opposed to most compasses, which point north. Just imagine there is a giant magnet at the top of the mountain.

www.ingramcontent.com/pod-product-compliance
Lightning Source LLC
Chambersburg PA
CBHW070657100426
42735CB00039B/2177